PRAISE
CLOSE ENOUGH TO
HEAR GOD BREATHE

This book has a heart that beats louder than most any book you'll ever read. But instead of leaving me breathless, *Close Enough to Hear God Breathe* left my breath and heart beating together and in sync with voices beyond myself. What higher compliment can you pay an author?

—LEONARD SWEET, BEST-SELLING AUTHOR,
PROFESSOR (DREW UNIVERSITY, GEORGE FOX UNIVERSITY),
AND CHIEF CONTRIBUTOR TO SERMONS.COM

My dear friend Greg does much more than remind us all that, indeed, one's heart is the wellspring of life. His shocking transparency, courageously tender words, and complete longing for God paint an indelible picture of what it means to truly know the quenching of a soul's thirst. I know no one—author, artist, orator, leader, servant, or friend—more consistent, or gifted, in mixing and spreading the colors of this glorious depiction, than my brother Greg. *Close Enough to Hear God Breathe* is not simply a wonderful book; it is a work of art.

—TIM HUFF, MULTI-AWARD-WINNING AUTHOR
AND ILLUSTRATOR OF *DANCING WITH DYNAMITE*,
BENT HOPE, AND *THE CARDBOARD SHACK BENEATH THE BRIDGE*;
AND FOUNDER AND EXECUTIVE DIRECTOR OF THE HOPE EXCHANGE

Greg Paul's writing always challenges me in surprising ways. He uses everyday experiences to stretch your thinking about God, faith, and community. In *Close Enough to Hear God Breathe*, Greg's writing is lyrical and his insights are profound. I recommend it.

—MARK SANBORN, NEW YORK TIMES BEST-SELLING AUTHOR
OF *THE FRED FACTOR* AND *UP, DOWN OR SIDEWAYS*

While theological writing is frequently obscure, biographical writing is often egocentric, leading us to the sad situation where we are not drawn very far into God's story or our own. However, as he has done in the past, Greg Paul has been sufficiently transparent about his own life so that we hear God's heartbeat. In the process we are impacted by a carefully woven tapestry of biography and theology.

—DR. ROD WILSON, PRESIDENT, REGENT COLLEGE

CLOSE
ENOUGH *to*
HEAR GOD
BREATHE

CLOSE ENOUGH *to* HEAR GOD BREATHE

The Great Story of Divine Intimacy

GREG PAUL

THOMAS NELSON
Since 1798

NASHVILLE   DALLAS   MEXICO CITY   RIO DE JANEIRO

Published in Nashville, Tennessee, by Thomas Nelson. Thomas Nelson is a registered trademark of Thomas Nelson, Inc.

Thomas Nelson, Inc., titles may be purchased in bulk for educational, business, fund-raising, or sales promotional use. For information, please e-mail SpecialMarkets@ThomasNelson.com.

Library of Congress Cataloging-in-Publication Data

Paul, Greg, 1958-
Close enough to hear God breathe / Greg Paul.
p. cm.
ISBN 978-1-4002-0300-0
1. Spiritual life--Christianity. I. Title.
BV4501.3.P3857 2011
248.4--dc22
2010047871

Printed in the United States of America

11 12 13 14 15 QG 6 5 4 3 2 1

For my family, of course—my parents, my
brothers, my children, and my Maggie.

CONTENTS

PROLOGUE

RAE AND ME, BREATHING

She's a beautiful young woman now, my daughter Rachel: tall and willowy, with long waves of mahogany hair; the kind of translucent, lightly freckled Irish skin that seems at times to be lit from within. Dark eyes, her mother's eyes, shining behind generous fronds of lash. Small pearly teeth, one of which is charmingly crooked, lending her frequent laugh an added visual giddiness. She didn't want to get that tooth fixed when she was of the age when such things are done. She liked her teeth the way they were, the way they are, thank you very much, and has never regretted it.

Rachel has three brothers. The two who are older, when she was a baby and would come crawling into their shared bedroom, among the carefully constructed toy villages or forts made of furniture and blankets, would shout, "Look out! Here comes Hurricane Rae!" The four of them are in their twenties now, and watching and listening to them when they're together is one of the great pleasures of my life.

They're tender and goofy, speaking in the layered codes of a lifetime of intimately shared experience. Family difficulties and sorrows have forged an unspoken loyalty among them. They giggle and poke each other like toddlers. They will deny it loudly, and joke about it when they read this, but they clearly adore one another.

It's axiomatic, I suppose, that a father has a special bond with his daughter, especially if she, like Rae, is the only one in a family of boys. The fact that she was the first girl born to the Paul family in more than sixty years might strengthen that some. (My father, who had three boys himself, then watched a steady stream of grandsons issue forth, didn't think it could be done. It's more than eighty years now, and two more boys, but she's still the only girl. And Rachel is utterly comfortable with that.)

But I think the real foundation of my particularly intimate relationship with Rae is that as an infant she would not nurse. Her three brothers did, enthusiastically. But she was indolent, uninterested, or maybe just stubborn. Try as she might, her mom couldn't get that long, skinny baby to latch on. The wonderful result was that Rachel was the only one of my four children I got to feed regularly as an infant.

I was a carpenter then. I'd arrive home weary and dirty,

have a quick shower and change into clean clothes, then take the baby while her brothers played and supper was being prepared.

After warming the bottle, Rae and I would start off in a big pine rocking chair with thick, tweedy cushions. While she wouldn't nurse, she took the bottle easily enough. Rocking gently. My daughter sucking greedily at first, then with an intermittent slack-mouthed draw; snuffling, burping, tiny sighs. Pink porcelain cheeks, fat violet eyelids at half-mast. A light brown milkweed fluff of hair on her round perfect head. The minor eruption down below.

Returning from the changing table, we move to the couch. I stretch out, my heels propped on the arm, head on a cushion, with the snugly wrapped package of baby on my chest. Rachel, my daughter, rising and falling gently with each breath I take. Her own breath is so light I can only hear it in those odd moments when the clatter from the kitchen and the chatter of my sons stop at the same time.

Looking down past my own cheeks, I can see the top of her head, the stub of nose peeking out. The pulse of the soft spot on her sweet little noggin slows down, and together we drift into sleep. Resting together on a greater chest, close enough to hear God breathing.

Part One

THE HEART OF THE MATTER

ONE

THE VOICE FROM ABOVE

At that time Jesus came from Nazareth in Galilee
and was baptized by John in the Jordan. As Jesus was
coming up out of the water, he saw heaven being torn
open and the Spirit descending on him like a dove.
And a voice came from heaven: "You are my Son,
whom I love; with you I am well pleased."

—FROM THE GOSPEL OF MARK, CHAPTER 1

There was a crowd, as usual, although dawn had barely broken. Hunkered on the banks of the river, scratching themselves absently and yawning, waiting for him to appear. Narrow ribbons of smoke stretched lazily upward in the still air from the ashes of a dozen small fires made and

7

tended through the cold night. They had missed out the day before, and decided to stay rather than making the long trek back to Jerusalem.

Most had no food, not having thought to bring any, or having eaten what little they had already. The few who did nibbled their crusts surreptitiously, not wanting to be besieged by their hungry neighbors. Some had no food simply because they had trudged through the wilderness to this spot by the Jordan instead of working that day, and so had no money to buy food anyway. They were a ragged bunch, mostly.

A furious rustling in the low, dense bushes lining the opposite bank—a pair of bony hands and one hairy leg emerged, thrust some branches aside, and the rest of the Baptist followed into view. A mutter ran through the crowd. The men stood up, the children stopped their games and stared. The Baptist stared back for a long moment, then nodded, apparently satisfied with what he saw, and turned his back on them.

His hair hung in matted hanks down his back. Everything about him seemed to be the same color as the desert floor. He undressed quickly, giving his ghastly camel-skin jerkin a flap—a cloud of ochre dust drifted away from it—before hanging it as carefully as if it were a linen robe on a branch of the bush from which he had appeared. As he bent to untie his sandals, he presented a pair of pale, scrawny cheeks so perfectly to his audience that a child guffawed. The Baptist gave no sign of noticing, but did procure a scrap of dirty cloth from a leather bag he had been carrying, and girded himself with it.

Seating himself on a rock, he drew the bag to him again, withdrew a small package, and unfolding it, began to eat the contents while gazing into the sky above their heads. He crunched away contentedly for a short while, then returned the cloth wrapper to the bag and licked each finger clean with a loud, delighted smacking sound.

"Locusts and honey," muttered an awestruck young boy to his brother.

The Baptist rose and, with a grin at the mob opposite, leapt into the river. It was only thigh deep, but he submerged himself, then floated face first to the surface. The mud he had disturbed bloomed creamily about him for a moment before the current shredded it and the river resumed its placid olive sheen.

Newcomers were beginning to arrive. They came from everywhere—not only from Jerusalem, but also from all the small towns of Judea, as well as those that dotted the shallow Jordan valley. As they drifted up, usually in small groups, the ones who had spent the night waiting moved quickly to line the bank, eager that the Baptist might choose them early in the day.

Finally standing upright, he began to preach. It was the same simple message they had heard repeatedly the day before. He kept up a running commentary as people waded into the river, as he embraced them, flung them backward into the muddy water, thrust any part of them that had not been submerged under the surface, then yanked them upright again. Always, it seemed, just as he had gotten to a point in his sermon when he could shout ". . . *forgiven!*"

9

The combination of the silty riverbed, the gentle current, and all the activity going on in one spot made it appear that he was slowly sinking. When the ground beneath his feet eroded enough that the water lapped around his ribs, he would clamber out of the hole and move eight or nine long steps upstream, the crowd shifting with him. Each time he did, he stopped baptizing for a while to preach in earnest, and to address the rumor that murmured incessantly through the steadily growing crowd.

"I am only baptizing you with water," he cried, "as a symbol that you have turned your faces away from your wicked ways, and toward God, and so that you will know he has washed you clean—your sins are forgiven! No, I am not Messiah—but he is coming soon! His kingdom is close enough to touch! He will sink you into the Holy Spirit, cleanse you with fire!"

It went on and on. Shortly before the sun reached its zenith, there was a disturbance at the back of the growing multitude on the riverbank. The tattered folk who had stayed the night shrank back from an advancing wedge of richly dressed men, some of them priests. They moved as if by right through the people who had been waiting for hours, making their way to the water's edge.

The Baptist didn't see them until they had reached it and stood there silently, half a dozen of them with their oiled beards, their hands secreted in wide sleeves across comfortable bellies.

He stopped speaking in mid-sentence and let go of the middle-aged woman he had just raised up from the river. She plunged back into it with a squawk, surged sputtering to the surface again, and clambered onto the bank casting murderous, unnoticed looks back at him.

The Baptist had been shouting his message so he could be heard, which makes any man sound angry, but when he found his voice to address the Pharisees, it was higher, harsher, and much, much louder than it had been all morning.

"*Snakes!*" he bellowed at them. They flinched as one man, but held their position. The Baptist derided their character, accused them of hypocrisy, and threatened them with judgment in rich terms that delighted the rest of the crowd. (Few things are more satisfying than seeing one's social and religious superiors trimmed a bit.) He had just finished telling them that they would be cut down like a barren fruit tree and thrown into the fire—a vein throbbing dangerously at his temple, the spittle flying—and was winding himself up to deliver even more extravagant condemnations when, it seemed, something distracted him.

Faltering to a stop, he turned to look squarely at the man a dozen steps upstream who had been waving circumspectly to him since shortly after he began his harangue. The Pharisees looked relieved, and dared to move a little. Their leader, a portly man with a silver beard and a tall turban, opened his mouth to speak, but the Baptist turned away and began splashing toward the waving man.

He was nothing special to look at. Just an ordinary man of ordinary height, complexion, and hair color. He was dressed just like everybody around him. He didn't seem to be with anyone—in fact, when they talked about it later, those around him who had so jealously guarded their positions at the river's edge weren't quite sure when he had arrived, or how he had made his way in front of them.

The ordinary man and the Baptist conversed quietly, oblivious to the fascinated mob around them. Who was he?

"A Galilean," said someone dismissively who was close enough to hear the accent.

"Ah!" said someone else. "That's his cousin, then. From Nazareth, but lives in Capernaum."

The two appeared to argue in a good-natured way, the man eventually cajoling the Baptist into some kind of agreement. He removed his outer garment and handed it to a young fellow in the crowd who, though he had never met the man before, received it and draped it over his arm as placidly as if he had followed him there for that express purpose. The man stepped into the river, found his footing, and plodded toward the middle, arm in arm with the Baptist.

For once, the Baptist was silent. He embraced the man with both arms, held him tight against his hollow chest, head bowed. Although he had been enthusiastically flinging people of all shapes and sizes into the water for hours, he now seemed reluctant, or perhaps even embarrassed. Gently, the Baptist lowered the man into the water, bending until his own arms were submerged to the biceps; a heartbeat's pause while he was completely out of sight, then the Baptist slowly raised him up again.

He sputtered and blew and rubbed his eyes as had everyone

else. He smiled and, placing a hand against the Baptist's hairy cheek, spoke a few inaudible words as if in blessing. Then he turned and began wading toward the bank.

It was all so ordinary, just like the man himself, and yet while he was being baptized, no one else had gone into the river to stand close to the Baptist, as they usually did, in hopes that he or she might be next. There was no rush of people into the water now, either. The crowd stood in a peculiar silence along the banks, unmoving, except for those few who stepped aside to allow him space to climb out. The air itself had become strangely still.

His eyes were turned skyward, over the heads of the people. Those nearest him could see that his lips were moving soundlessly. The Baptist, forgotten for the moment, stood motionless behind him, his hands dangling in the hip-deep water.

There was a tearing sound from above—thunder, perhaps, is what some thought later. A curious purplish cloud formation—which looked like a gash across what had been, as far as anyone could remember, an empty sky only moments before—seemed to flutter open. A dark spot descending quickly from the gash—the "gash" seemed strangely near for a cloud—resolved into a dove, a very ordinary-looking dove, but with it came a gentle breeze, gentle and warm and beautifully moist in the desert air.

The man was smiling broadly, raising his eyebrows and looking up without tilting his head, as well he might, since the dove had landed upon it and sat there cooing comfortably. Several people laughed out loud. He nodded at the ones closest to him who had laughed (the dove undisturbed by the motion), sharing their delight.

The gash in the clouds rippled repeatedly, as a man's heart beats, and each time there was another puff of the warm breeze. As if the sky was breathing upon them. The sky breathed a word into them, all those people standing there looking at the man. With each breath a phrase:

"This is my son. My beloved. I am pleased with him."

They all heard it, though it was so quiet it might have been easily missed. They knew the voice was speaking about the ordinary man, the man who looked like them. Many also heard the breeze speak directly to the man. Hearing it as they did, like the breath within their own bodies, they wondered if it also spoke to each of them:

"You are my child—my son, my daughter. I love you.
And I am pleased with you."

TWO

THE HEART OF THE MATTER

If every story has certain pivotal moments, moments that clarify everything that has gone before and set up everything that's to come, surely this is such a moment in the story of God's relationship with humanity! This is the moment when the Word-Made-Flesh appears to the world: God's voice, and everything he wants to say to us with it, given a completely accessible, fully human form and substance. The Father, Son, and Holy Spirit are tangibly—and uniquely[1]—present at this extraordinary event: the voice from above, the man on the riverbank, and the spirit descending "like a dove" from voice to man, connecting them visibly. Here, by the words he chooses, God reveals both his unique relationship with Jesus, and that he intends to relate to us also as a parent does to his or her child.

If the people standing on the bank of the river that day had known before the sky was torn open that the ordinary-looking man coming out of the water was God, I wonder what kind of introduction they might have expected? How about, "Introducing . . . The One! The Beginning and the End, the Creator and Sustainer of all things, King of kings and Judge of the nations, Supreme Commander of the Armies of Heaven. He holds the keys of Death and Hell . . ."

That would certainly have gotten my attention. How fascinating, how significant it is that God spoke of and to Jesus in the most tender and intimate terms instead: "*I want you to meet my boy . . .*"

As the writer of the letter to the Hebrews put it, "In the past God spoke to our forefathers through the prophets at many times and in various ways, but in these last [most recent] days he has spoken to us by his Son"[2]—or, as a literal translation would render it, "he has spoken to us *in Son.*" That is, in the language of "Son," the language of intimate, familial relationship.

When Jesus asks John to baptize him, the Baptist is understandably uncomfortable with the notion. Exactly how much he knows about Jesus' true identity before the baptism takes place is unclear, but he certainly realizes that it's Jesus who ought to be baptizing him. After all, of what sins shall Jesus repent?

Jesus says, in essence, "Yes, you're right. But let it roll, because this—my identifying with all the yokels gawking at us from the riverbank—this is how all of God's profound, perfect goodness will be delivered to humanity—to the whole cosmos!"

In this crucial moment, Jesus is not only God-with-Us; he is also, mysteriously and wonderfully, One-of-Us. He stands in that muddy river, disappears beneath its surface, and rises both as a representative of all humanity, and as its salvation. He represents both God and me.

And so, when the Voice from heaven speaks, the message is not only for the unique Son of God, but is also for every human being. This is "the true light that gives light to every man."[3]

When I got through reading the three gospel versions of the story, perhaps in several translations, and past comparing them and imagining the scene, checking the specific meanings of a few key words, browsing through reference works and so on, and put the book down, and sat quietly listening for the sound of God breathing, I heard him say to me—to me!—the same thing he said to Jesus that day.

"You're my child. My beloved. My pleasure."

This is the heart of the matter. This is the message that blows quietly, sweetly through the whole Bible. It's easy to lose it in the strictures of law, the violent stories of the people of Israel, the doom-laden pronouncements of the prophets, or the near-psychedelic foretelling of future events. It's so tender, so gentle, that it's easy to miss it blowing through my own little life story, with all its dramas and distractions.

There are a thousand other voices, most of them much louder and more insistent, that have other things to say about who I am. They say things that are demeaning or discouraging. Sometimes they say things that make me so proud of myself that I forget God is whispering his beautiful message to everyone else too. Sometimes they speak words that cut or bruise my soul, telling me I am unlovely and unlovable—a message I am unaccountably ready to believe. They may be the voices of people close to me, the culture around me, the advertising I can't escape, religion, education, or of my own innate pride or insecurities.

There are so many of these other voices, and they are so constant that I can't escape them. I need new "ears" to be able to hear what God has to say. As with the people of the Baptist's day, it begins with coming to the river of God's grace and being submerged in it. Dying to an old life, an old way of hearing, and rising again to a new life, which can only come as a gift from above. Confessing my sins—admitting that I am too broken to live the identity for which God made me. Repenting—changing the course of my thinking about myself, my world, and my Creator.

My child. My beloved. My pleasure.

It seems as if it should be easy to hear these words and believe them, but it's not. An entire life of discipleship cannot fully mine these three simple expressions. It's the work of a lifetime just to begin to truly believe them.

Because I was blessed with parents who were devout Christians, I began to follow Jesus when I was still only a little boy. For a long time, I sought specific guidance from God, through prayer and Scripture mostly, about where to go, what to do, and how and when to do it, and much, much more. In times past and in many different ways, he often gave me the instructions I was seeking, or at least I felt he did. But now, in these recent days, he speaks to me "in Son." Whispering through every Scripture, and into the intimate details of my own daily experience—for it is his life he is breathing into me, and my life he wants to redeem.

Over and over, as I lay my head on his chest, he says the same thing to me, knowing how hard it is for me to hear and believe:

"My child. My beloved. My pleasure."

THREE

THE GREAT STORY

Ⓐll my life, I've loved stories. My children did too—
is there a child who doesn't? Through the years, I
read aloud all the books of the *Narnia Chronicles*, *The
Hobbit*, and *The Lord of the Rings* to my kids. Curled up on the
couch or on their beds, we got lost together in those fabulous
tales. We read *Kidnapped*, *The Black Arrow*, and *Treasure Island*. On
a driving trip through Nebraska, Wyoming, and the Dakotas,
down through Utah and into Arizona, we plowed through a
slew of Louis L'Amour's books as the very landscape of those
punchy little cowboy yarns slid past the van windows.

The magic of a story is that it enfolds you, carries you away
to a place you've never been before (even if it's set in your
hometown), and yet is so full of familiar touchstones—sights,

sounds, scents, longing, fears, disappointments, and triumphs—that you can imagine yourself bearing the awful weight of the Ring, bracing yourself against the heave of the deck of a brigantine under full canvas, or feeling the delicious, warm breath of the Lion in your face. My children and I inhabited those stories together. A good story allows you to admit your fears, and hope that you might be a hero in the face of them.

I'm not sure why adults so often lose the art of "entering" a story in written form. Maybe the visual power of movies, so easily received, seduces us into allowing our imaginations to atrophy. Maybe the remnants of our modernist history cultivate within us the idea that imagination is childish, that information is the proper pursuit of the adult mind.

Our loss.

I still love novels and would rather read them than philosophy, theology, "real" history, psychology, or any other form of fact-based writing. I think I've learned more about the human condition—and the scope of the human spirit—from novels than from any other form of writing. (Just as I have learned more about real faith and true spiritual growth from my street-involved friends, as they have shared their stories with me, than I have from any of the sources that are supposed to convey such understanding.)

Jesus did most of his teaching in the form of storytelling for a reason. We remember stories more easily and more completely than we do facts. We assimilate stories differently, bringing to them the shades of understanding made possible by our own experiences, finding something new each time we approach even one that has long been familiar. A story is like a multifaceted jewel, giving off a different light each time it is turned. The famous story of the prodigal son, for instance, has a fresh power each time I listen to it, imagining myself successively in the role of the prodigal, the faithful but resentful son who stayed home, the loving father.

The Bible, first and foremost, is a story. Like all great stories, it contains many smaller stories within it, plus a great deal of factual information, as well as philosophy, theology, sociology, anthropology, politics, and economics. But approaching it as a treatise on any of those subjects is to miss the heart of the matter as completely as if one read *Great Expectations* as an essay on the Industrial Revolution.

Every story has a structure. Most simply, a beginning, a middle, and an end—although, as Bilbo recognizes in *The Lord of the Rings*, the story never *really* ends, and there is always something that came before the beginning of any tale we might tell.

There is an old, simple way of describing God's plan for creation—the unfolding of the Great Story of his dreams for the noble future of all he made. I'm not sure when it originated, but part of it was expressed by neo-Calvinists in the mid- to late 1800s[1]—the description, that is, not the plan! (Many people of various faiths do seem to think—or at least act as if—God is following their plan, rather than the other way around.) Realizing that the phrase will describe me before long, I have a growing affection for things that are "old and simple."

According to this description of the plot of the Great Story, there are four movements, divisions, or epochs: *creation, fall, redemption*, and *consummation*. These movements are sequential, but they also overlap. Humanity, for instance, is still God's creation, but is "fallen"; although fallen, humanity is (or at least individuals are) in the process of being redeemed; within the redemptive process are the seeds of the final consummation.

Creation refers to the time and state of everything God made before Adam and Eve were driven from Eden. Everything in the cosmos was as God intended it to be; it was perfect, as such, and he regarded it as good.

The *Fall* refers not only to Adam and Eve messing up things by eating the forbidden fruit but also to the consequent effect of sin on all of creation, including the state of alienation between God and humanity.

Redemption refers to the process by which God is "buying back" his own creation, and not only returning it to its former state of goodness, but raising it even higher. This is made possible, mysteriously, by the death and resurrection of his dear Son, Jesus. Even more mysteriously, this redemption apparently works backward in time as well as forward. For instance, the most ancient of biblical writers, Job, placed his faith in one he called "my Redeemer,"[2] and as a result was regarded by God as righteous.

Consummation refers to the final "summing up" of all things, and the ultimate reconciling of all creation into right relationship with its Creator. This is not merely a return to the garden of Eden, but a quantum leap forward into a new, profoundly intimate, and endless relationship with God, excepting only those who choose not to receive his gift of grace through Christ.

These are the basic "movements" or "acts" of the Great Story. Scores of books have been written about the import of each of these movements, of course, but for our purposes they will serve as a simple "plot outline" of Scripture and history, helping us to correlate our own little stories to the great one.

✠

I was out for brunch recently with my eldest son, Caleb, my daughter, Rachel, and Rachel's boyfriend, and got to telling stories about the kids when they were little. That sweet little bundle who would burble her way into sleep on my chest became a terror when she got a little older. I regaled our table with tales of how, when she hit the terrible twos, Rachel would begin to scream when we tried to put her to bed. I'm not talking about a little moaning for fifteen or twenty minutes, I mean she screamed— a bloodcurdling, full-throated, keening, banshee-on-steroids wail—for hours at a time. After a few weeks of this, her poor parents were so bemused and aggravated that they began to worry they would hurt her in their frustration. I installed a privacy lock on her bedroom door, with the locking mechanism on the outside. We'd plant her in bed, hurry out, and bolt the door behind us.

Visitors would smile tolerantly at first, while Rachel's personal air raid siren was winding up, then look puzzled and a little unnerved as the volume and intensity increased, *while the poor little thing's parents ignored her entirely.* Finally they'd ask, "Um, aren't you going to look in on her?" A look of dumb shock at the blithe response—"Oh, that? No, she does that every night . . ."

My brunch audience chuckled at the tale. I went on to tell about the time the house went silent while she and I were home alone. I found her waiting for me in the basement with a jar of paint thinner from which she had removed the soaking brush— waiting for me to see her and shout "No!" before taking a big drink of it. And then I told about the time Caleb, only four or five years old, stepped around me just as I swung a souvenir bat at a bouncing tennis ball. I whacked him straight across the forehead, and he went down like a bag of bricks, instantly pale, stunned, and immobile. For a few horrid moments, I thought I had seriously damaged my beloved son. We laughed about that one, too, making the expected jokes about how he's never been the same since.

As I told these and other hoary old family stories, mostly about disasters survived, Caleb and Rachel supplied missing bits. Maybe they were just humoring the old man, but it seems to me that they actually enjoyed the reciting of their own lore.

Young children—children of any age!—often love to hear about things that happened to them when they were littler still, things they may not even remember. The recounting of their personal lore roots them in their family's history, affirms who they are, and conveys both the present delight and the fervent hope of their parents (usually the storytellers) for a bright future. It lets them know that their own personal story is part of a much larger one.

"Let the little children come to me, and do not hinder them," Jesus told his disciples, "for the kingdom of God belongs to such as these. I tell you the truth, anyone who will not receive the kingdom of God like a little child will never enter it."[3]

Then he took the children in his arms and whispered blessings in their ears.

I want to hear the Story in this way, with the words floating on the very breath of God.

I want to know that my own little story is rooted in the Great Story of the Eternal Father and His children, and that it matters. I want to see that my own faults and failures are reflected in those of others, that I am not alone, that my neediness does not ultimately doom me; that, astonishingly, I am precious. I want to submit my nearsighted interpretations of the complex world in which I live; and the vagaries of its history, science, economics, politics, and religion; and my hopes and fears for its future, to the deep, broad current on which they ride. I want to *know* the heart of the matter.

"All scripture is God-breathed,"[4] Paul says, and he goes on to describe how valuable Scripture is for a variety of purposes that sound very much like child-rearing. The Greek and Hebrew words used in the Bible for *breath* derive from the same words as the Greek and Hebrew terms for *spirit*.[5] It's a pun, of sorts. The term Paul uses is made up of two Greek words jammed together: *theo* (God) and *pneustos* (breathed or spirited).

All Scripture is God-spirited. His spirit is flowing through all of it, Paul suggests, as subtle and quiet and necessary-to-life as a person breathing. If you listen as you read and catch the rhythm of his breathing, he will teach you, rebuke you when you need it, set you on the right path again, and train you up to his own character—the way a parent does a child in a thousand tiny ways each day, hardly noticed, until, years later, the child has become a man or a woman, equipped in every way to live a good and fruitful life.

Two things are necessary for me to be able to hear someone breathing: I must be quiet and I must be close.

Paul is telling me that when I learn to hear God breathing in Scripture, it will be rest to my soul. Not merely an academic exercise or a dogmatic wrangle. And I will know that God is very near, perhaps particularly when I'm stumped by a mystery I cannot penetrate. Amazingly, I find that when I listen carefully enough to the sound of that breathing in Scripture, it echoes also through the stories of my own life.

When I read the Bible, my main purpose is not to learn facts about the writers, the culture of the time, the empiric provability of statements made, or rules and regulations for living. It's not even to learn facts about God or Jesus, although all of these things will aid my purpose if they are not ends in themselves. When I seek to know a thing by mastering the minutiae about it, I risk destroying the integrity of the whole of it. I may learn a great deal about the anatomy of a frog by dissecting it, but by the time I'm done, it's no longer a frog.

I want to "hear" the story God is telling me—the Great Story of his passionate love for all humanity and all creation. Wisdom is being able also to find my own personal little story within that big one. I want my spirit to vibrate at the same frequency as the Spirit.

Listening to the Story ought to be like lying on my Father's chest, a vulnerable, beloved infant, rich with potential, the focus of his dreams for a great and noble future. Rising and falling with each breath, the gentle sound of it in my ears, the warm tickle of it on my head.

The beating of his great heart supporting mine. Listen . . .

Part Two

CREATION

FOUR

A GOOD LIKENESS

My Child:

Then God said, "Let us make [humanity] in our image, in our likeness, and let them rule over the fish of the sea and the birds of the air, over the livestock, over all the earth, and over all the creatures that move along the ground."

So God created man in his own image, and in the image of God he created him; male and female he created them.

God blessed them and said to them, "Be fruitful and increase in number . . ."

God saw all that he had made, and it was very good.

. . . the LORD God formed the man from the dust

of the ground and breathed into his nostrils the breath
of life, and the man became a living being.

—FROM GENESIS, CHAPTERS 1 AND 2

When my four children are together, there's no mis-
taking that they are siblings. That they all have dark
hair and dark eyes is part of it, but there's much
more to it than that. They're all adults now and very distinctly
individual, yet there's some underlying similarity that is hard to
define. This similarity perhaps has as much to do with bearing
and expression as it does with the way they actually look.

When they were little, one person would say to me, "He
looks so much like you!" Often another would say, about the
same child, "Oh, he's the spit and image of his mother." Both
were right, I suppose. Eventually, I concluded that any person's
opinion of whether one of my sons or my daughter looked
more like me or their mom depended on which of the parents
was better known to that person.

I had always thought my son Jesse looked least like his
dad. Then one day when Jesse was about eighteen, my old
friend Kevin, a very talented artist, gave me a drawing he
had done many years before. It hangs on my office wall now:
Pencil crayon on board, so brightly colored and finely detailed
that it looks like an acrylic painting. A young man wearing
a red leather motorcycle jacket, his hands in the pockets of

his jeans, stands looking straight at the viewer out of hooded eyes. His head has a characteristic tilt, his shoulders a very particular set.

It could have been a fresh portrait of Jesse—the color of the hair, the set of the jaw, the stance that mixed self-consciousness and cool, the direct stare from beneath a slightly lowered brow. It is, of course, a picture of me at eighteen.

When I listen for the quiet voice of God my Father breathing through the stories of Creation, I can't help but remember my own experiences as a young parent. I watched with wonder as my own children came into being—the products, in part, of my own body—and grew into being both distinctly themselves and the consistent (sometimes unnervingly so) reflection of my own being.

One of the peculiarities of the Hebrew language is that, unlike most modern languages, nouns can be singular, dual, or plural. That is, a noun may indicate one single thing, or two specifically (dual), or three or more (plural). English, of course, is only able to indicate singular or plural—one, or two, or more. The word for God in the quote at the head of this chapter, and throughout Genesis chapter 1, is plural. In other words, the story is relating a conversation between the three members of the Trinity.

It makes me think of the kind of excited discussions many couples have as they contemplate having children. Do you think we're ready to have kids? Can we afford it? How many do you want? Do we have enough space—will we have to move? I really hope we have a girl! Well, I don't care as long as he or she is healthy . . . What will we name her? Bottle or breast? Cloth or disposable?

The questions are endless. Beneath them is a deeper question that is rarely discussed. Why do so many people have such a profound desire to have children anyway? The pleasure of begetting them is no longer an answer, if ever it was. Gone are the days when a young couple had as many children as quickly as possible because they would become, literally, a homegrown workforce for the family business and a hedge against infirmity and old age. Kids are costly in time, money, energy, emotions, freedom, physical space, and much more.

In my community it is tragically common for women to bear children they will not be able to keep because they are homeless or struggling with addictions, mental illness, or other serious dysfunctions. One friend of mine, a beautiful young aboriginal woman, has had nine children while living on the street. As I was writing this chapter, she delivered another little boy. She just recently turned thirty-two. All of her children have been taken at birth by the authorities, and she and the baby's father are all but certain to lose this child too. When that happens, both of them will go into another self-destructive tailspin, punishing themselves for failing yet again at this fundamental human endeavor.

In a poignant, backhanded sort of way, even their heart-breaking story carries echoes for me of what God is saying in the creation story. In the face of every grim reality, in the midst of their deep, deep brokenness, in a hope so faint that it can only be called fantasy, they conceive children for the same basic reason that most other parents do, and for the same reason that God created us.

Listen to the conversation in Genesis chapter 1:

We've created all this other amazing stuff—sky, sea, solar systems, mountains and stars and plants and animals, an entire universe of wonder—now let's make something that looks just like us.

Yes, some one *who looks just like us!*

Oh, someone who will delight in doing the things we do—creating stuff, growing it, enjoying it.

Let's make two, so they really *look like us—strong and bold, tender and wise, living in wildly intimate, loving, complementary relationship. Delighting in each other so much that they, too, will want to create their own offspring—become three!—reliving over and over the way we've created them . . .*

We don't usually talk about it, perhaps we're not even all that conscious of it, but what we desire, whether we are relatively healthy, balanced people living "normal" lives, or we are so broken that we are responding to a dim, primal longing, is to reproduce our own selves. To have someone who is part of me, so close that I will not hesitate to lavish upon that person the very best of all that I am and have. Someone who, as he or she grows, will become more like me, and at the same time more clearly him or herself.

We come face-to-face with this desire at those moments when, ruefully, or with hearts full of pride, we recognize ourselves in our children.

My eldest son, Caleb, was only four or five at the time. I can still remember it clearly, although nothing much happened and it was more than twenty years ago. He was sitting on the bottom step of the stairway to the second floor of our house, explaining something to me in the most serious tones. I crouched in front of him, only half listening—while he was deeply in earnest about his subject. It was, from an adult point of view, of no great consequence. I don't even remember what it was. He wasn't asking my opinion or seeking an answer. What mattered to him was that I was listening attentively as he spoke.

Really, I was looking at him much more intently than I was listening. In that moment I recognized him as beautiful, in the way a parent or a doting childless aunt does—the most beautiful child in the world! (Except, of course, for his siblings, each the most beautiful child in his or her own unique way.) A thick swatch of glossy dark brown hair. Very straight eyebrows across a high alabaster forehead. A short straight nose, lightly freckled. Round pink cheeks and a busy little set of red lips. He still had trouble with the letter *L*, pronouncing his own name "Cayub."

He held me with his gaze, his head tilted slightly down so that he peered at me from beneath that level brow. His voice was low, steady, grave. He raised his right hand, extended the tiny index finger, and poked it toward my chest to emphasize each salient point he made.

Holy cow! I thought. *That's me!*

He had said or done nothing in particular to make me proud, nothing that would have produced in anyone else anything more than quiet amusement, but my heart nearly burst. Despite the fact that not every aspect of the image was complementary, the reflection of myself in my little boy thrilled me.

It's exactly this kind of delight, a delight in *me*, that the Father breathes into my soul when I read that as he looked at humanity and all he had made for us, "he saw that it was *very* good."[1] The image of the Father in me is indelible, clouded though it may be, and because of it, I am infinitely precious to him.

Nothing can eradicate this image in me, I who am also three-in-one—body, soul, spirit. Not "the Fall," nor my own misbehavior; nothing. Nevertheless, I have a tough time recognizing this image in the mirror. So often I don't like what I see, and sometimes with good reason. Even at my most egotistical, some more rational part of me knows that I am small, unimportant, and just not "very good."

It's a significant work of faith to believe that my Father does see me as "very good." I have to be very still and listen very carefully in order to sort out the contradictory voices (my own and others') and receive what he is saying.

Unless I can actually hear the Father saying to me, *You are my child; you bear my image and will grow up to look like me,* I can't truly embrace who he made me to be. I'll grow, alright, but into some other image, a cartoon of the self I was meant to be, produced by the battle between my pride and my insecurities, and colored by the thousand other voices that clamor to tell me who I should be.

It was true for Adam, and it's true for me: I am, until the Father breathes life into me, a man-shaped pile of earth, rich with potential, but powerless to realize it.

The message that I am a child of God, made in his image and intended to grow up to fulfill it, sounds regularly through the Great Story, as calmly consistent as the rise and fall of my own chest.

One of the earliest names of God, usually translated "the Almighty," would be better translated "the All-Sufficient." Most of the earliest uses of this name, in Job and Genesis, are connected with the promise of blessing through the gift of children; it conveys the entire sufficiency of a nursing mother for her infant. Some translators actually say that it means "the Breasted One." He is not only Father, but Mother too! It's worth reflecting on what has compelled English translators to so consistently render the Hebrew word thus, offering a view of God that leans heavily toward overwhelming dominance, rather than the kind of strength that willingly and lovingly gives itself to supplying the needs of a vulnerable, dependent baby.

Early in Solomon's Proverbs, the Holy Spirit is characterized as a wise woman (*Sophia* in the Greek version, usually translated *Wisdom* in English) who cries out words of warning and invitation in the streets. It's part of the setup for the rest of the Proverbs, addressed over and over with beautiful tenderness to "my son." Perhaps the inference from these and many other passages is that the Trinity is a kind of holy family: a Father

God, a Mother Spirit, and the Son. And this Family reproduces itself, as families generally do, in the family of humanity.

God's promises of blessing to the patriarchs are all rooted in the promise of children. The release of the "children of Israel" from slavery in Egypt comes to pass when the blood of a lamb protects the firstborn son of each Israelite household.

In hundreds of passages throughout the poetic and prophetic books, God describes himself as a father to those who will turn to him, and to those who have been abandoned by their own fathers or governments.

A child is proclaimed as the one to whom God will give ultimate government, as well as the titles Wonderful Counselor, Mighty God, and Prince of Peace.

The child himself is born—as poor, weak, and apparently insignificant as any other, and yet the fulcrum of history. When the child grows up and speaks, as often he does, about his relationship to God, he insists on calling him Father, to the great consternation of the religious authorities of the day.

The kingdom of heaven, the Son proclaims, is for those who will come as little children.

Paul jubilantly tells anxious Roman Christians, "You did not receive a spirit that makes you a slave again to fear, but you received the Spirit of sonship"—*it was not fear he breathed into you, but the understanding of a new and intimate relationship*—"and by him we cry, 'Abba!'"—the equivalent of *Da-da!* And in case we're not getting the point, he goes on to make it crystal clear: "The Spirit himself testifies with our spirit that we are God's children."[2]

The writer of the letter to the Hebrews, drawing a picture of Jesus "bringing many sons to glory"—that is, presenting me and my brothers and sisters to the Father—quotes the Son as saying, "Here am I, and the children God has given me."[3]

"Beloved," John says, "now we are children of God; and it has not yet been revealed what we shall be, but we know that when He is revealed, we shall be like Him, for we shall see Him as He is."[4]

It's only a whisper at first. But when I still myself and filter out the competing sounds, the volume grows.

FIVE

Happiness Is a Hot Shower

My Love:

How great is the love the Father has lavished on us,
that we should be called children of God! And that is
what we are!

And so we know and rely on the love God has for
us. God is love. Whoever lives in love lives in God,
and God in him.

—from 1 John, chapters 3 and 4

My father was known by some as a tough, gruff man,
and for good reason. His mother died when he was
four years old, in the early part of the Dirty Thirties,

leaving my grandfather with four young children. Although my grandfather would later marry a woman my father came to love and revere as his "real mother," Dad's only memory of his birth mother was of her lying in a coffin in the front room of the family home.

My grandfather had been a master carpenter, but left the trade to pursue a ministry as an itinerant preacher—not exactly a ticket to the good life during the Depression.

For several years, the family subsisted largely on the sacks of potatoes and onions, along with the occasional chicken or a few eggs, left on their front porch by kind neighbors in their small town. Although Dad was the youngest of the kids, because he was the only boy he was routinely instructed by a chorus of three older sisters and a housekeeper as to the manly chores he was expected to fulfill each time his father disappeared on another preaching junket. Every morning before leaving for school, at only six or seven years of age, he was expected to pump and haul the day's water, as well as haul enough wood to keep the kitchen stove going.

Growing up, he did all the stuff you see children do now only in developing nations or in old black-and-white movies: making deliveries by bicycle for the local grocery store after school; laboring on a nearby farm during the summer months; as a skinny sixteen-year-old, slugging one-hundred-pound sacks of flour at the local mill. But he was much more than just a hard-working small-town laborer. He had a good brain, and kept his eye on the future. He saved up, with his family's encouragement, and ultimately went off to university. It was an uncommon achievement for a boy from a family that was often struggling to get by.

He graduated in 1949—the same year as many returning World War II vets—with a degree in chemical engineering, one of the most demanding disciplines at the University of Toronto. He had worn just one suit to class every day for four years, and had paid his way by painting houses. Because he was competing with war vets, it proved impossible to get a job in his field right away. He spent another year and a half painting, cycling from site to site with a ladder slung between his bicycle and a mate's, paint cans and drop cloths secured carefully to the ladder.

I learned these things from him in bits and pieces through the years, and never once did I hear a note of self-pity or resentment.

He was a man of intelligence, diligence, and cast-iron integrity. To the end of his days, few things gave him greater pleasure than physical work. Small wonder that he became a success in the business world, taking a small company teetering on the verge of bankruptcy, turning it into a solid national concern, and spinning several other successful companies off from it. Today that company is going stronger than ever, under the direction of my oldest brother, John.

Small wonder, too, that Dad had trouble empathizing with people who couldn't get the job done or even order their own lives. His crustiness regarding failures or perspectives he didn't understand made his generosity to many of those same people all the more surprising. It was his mental, emotional, and spiritual rigor, his physical vitality, the capacity to focus narrowly and with great tenacity on the task at hand that propelled him to success as what many would describe as the classic self-made man.[1]

But those same characteristics sometimes also meant that he was not so adept at expressing the warmer emotions. Used to being the boss and having had to make all the hard decisions on his own, he was not inclined to accommodate disagreement. My brother David, the middle son, has his own stories about that. He left home while still in his teens, ended up in England, and didn't come back to visit for twenty-five years.

When I was in my early twenties, I dared to challenge some deeply held doctrines of the church in which my father and my mother had raised me. To make a long and painful story short, my convictions ultimately would not allow me to stay in that church (I was, after all, my father's son); my father's convictions could not allow him to approve. A rift opened up between us that lasted for many years, although we continued to spend time together at family events.

My father had never found it easy to speak tender or affirming words. Now it hardly seemed possible between us. Both of us were angry and hurt at what we perceived as the other's rejection. What conversations we did have tended to stick to subjects safe and mundane, and almost never broached the spiritual things that mattered most to both of us.

When he was about seventy, he experienced chest pains—while clearing snow from the driveway so that he and my mother could attend church—that landed him in hospital. It turned out much later that it was only a virus, but an allergy to the nitroglycerin the doctors kept administering prompted the symptoms of repeated heart attacks.

When I visited him in the ICU, both of us believed his heart was badly damaged and that he might die. I had determined to say the things I had always put off, and did: that I loved him, that I knew I had hurt him deeply by leaving, and regretted the pain I had caused him and my mother. That it was him, more than anyone else, who had taught me as a child and young man to listen to what God says through Scripture, and obey it. That I was still trying to do exactly that.

My father looked at me with glistening eyes. Although he was capable of speech, he was unable to respond. He couldn't squeeze a single word out, although he did squeeze my hand. I left with the realization that if he couldn't say what he felt then, he just simply couldn't say it at all.

Within a few weeks, he was fine. He returned to his usual ridiculously high level of health and energy, and we never spoke of that time in the ICU.

I had longed to hear from him an unqualified "I love you." It seemed to me that if I performed some task flawlessly, he remained silent, but if I made a mistake or goofed off, I heard about it endlessly. I'm sure it looked to some distant observers as if I didn't give a toss about what my father thought of me. But it seemed to me that, from the time I became a teenager, some dim corner of my psyche had been seeking fruitlessly for his approval.

It took me a long time to realize my father had, in fact,

often expressed his love for me—and his blessing—in terms that were, for him, quite eloquent.

He had made it possible for us to buy our first home, by giving us a large, interest-free loan at a time (the early eighties) when mortgages were nibbling at 20 percent. He made it possible for us to add to and renovate that little house when Kelly, our fourth child, was on the way. He helped me with the construction and, in a return to his early vocation, painted the exterior. He had built an addition on his vacation property, a cottage on a Muskoka lake, so that my family would have a place of our own there—no small feat, with four very active children.

He helped me buy a truck and hired me for projects at his home and his company when an economic downturn in the late eighties made it necessary for me to start my own carpentry business. By the early nineties, I had left the carpentry behind and begun working as a missionary in the downtown core of Toronto, among street-involved people. Eventually, this work grew into a community called Sanctuary, and it's still home to me.

In those early days, as I was struggling along on a meager and indefinite income, my father and my mother made it possible for us to buy a van and renovate the kitchen in our new-old house downtown. My father didn't seem much interested in supporting the ministry I was starting, but was eager to make sure my family lived in a good place. All these things and many more, I have come to realize, were my father's ways of telling me that he loved me.

⳨

I often don't find it easy to recognize my heavenly Father's ways of communicating his love, either. I rarely have that warm sense of his tender, intimate presence, nor, however much I long for it, do I hear the actual sound of his voice saying, "I love you."

Neither does the creation account in the first couple of chapters of Genesis recount God saying those words to Adam and Eve. But the care and extravagance with which he built their "home"—the world itself!—speaks to me with the utmost eloquence of his eternal commitment and unfailing love for them. With each successive day's creative accomplishment, and the proclamation that it was good, I can hear his delight in preparing a magnificent home, including all that was needed for their sustenance, for the pair whom he had created for the very purpose of love.

And not only for Adam and Eve.

I began writing this book on a two-week retreat, kindly and very generously provided by my friends Miller and Terri. On the first day, I sat in a chair in the sun overlooking the Pacific Ocean. Where the high cerulean dome of cloudless sky bent down to the sea, the brilliant sunshine had bleached it to the palest blue. The calm, perfect union of sky and water at the horizon line gave mysterious birth to wild, racing waves that ran laughing up the beach below, until they were spent and retired with a sigh beneath their rushing brothers.

God is *love*, John says.

As I asked my Father to allow me enough peace in the coming days to hear him breathing, I became aware of a breeze whispering over my face, steady but too light to notice unless I was sitting quite still. And the sun, its warmth growing as I quieted and my own breathing slowed, kissing my upturned face.

The one who loves, abides in God, and God in him.

The God who is love has by that love created the "house" I live in—every tree, every blade of grass, every diamond-studded wave proclaims it. I take it for granted, ignore it, abuse it. Only rarely do I see it for what it is. Living in this love is the closest thing there is in this present world to living in the garden of Eden, and the closest thing to the promise of the glory on ahead.

My story is an echo of the Great Story. My father's love is my Father's love, and every love is his love. God made Adam and Eve for each other, so that they could dwell in love—his love in them, through them, to them, binding them together. He made them for love because he is love, and although I waste so much time and energy seeking cheap copies of it, he made me for love too.

In my earliest memory of my father, I am, I think, three or four years old. He holds me in his arms and my face is very close to his. His black hair is plastered to his forehead by the water streaming from the showerhead behind me, the water drumming a tattoo on my back. I can see his eyes, blue as a northern lake, looking right into mine. He is holding my hand, sticking my small fingers into his mouth, blowing on them, making me giggle. He picks up a bar of soap, and as he begins to scrub my back, I put my arms around his neck and my cheek against his. My little chest resting on his broad, smooth one. His cheek is rough with stubble; I can feel his arm beneath my bum, effortlessly holding me up. He leans closer to the showerhead; his mouth is near my ear, and I can hear him blowing the water away as it streams over his face.

This is where I want to abide. In the arms of my Father, his heart beating against mine. In the beautiful, rich, enduring world of his love.

SIX

HAMMER AND NAILS

My Pleasure:

God blessed them and said to them, "I give you every
seed-bearing plant on the face of the whole earth and
every tree that has fruit with seed in it. They will be
yours for food. And to all the beasts of the earth and all
the birds of the air and all the creatures that move on
the ground—everything that has the breath of life in
it—I give every green plant for food." And it was so.

God saw all that he had made, and it was very
good . . .

Now the LORD God had formed out of the ground
all the beasts of the field and all the birds of the air.
He brought them to the man to see what he would
name them; and whatever the man called each living

creature, that was its name. So the man gave names to all the livestock, the birds of the air and all the beasts of the field.

But for Adam no suitable helper was found. So the LORD God caused the man to fall into a deep sleep; and while he was sleeping, he took one of the man's ribs and closed up the place with flesh. Then the LORD God made a woman from the rib he had taken out of man, and he brought her to the man.

The man said, "This is now bone of my bones and flesh of my flesh; she shall be called 'woman,' for she was taken out of man."

For this reason a man will leave his father and mother and be united to his wife, and they will become one flesh.

The man and his wife were both naked, and they felt no shame.

—FROM GENESIS, CHAPTERS 1 AND 2

A theology that begins with the "total depravity of man" is a theology that starts the story off in "Chapter Two."

John Calvin didn't mean by "total depravity" that every human being is psychotic or sociopathic. He meant that every human being is sinful through and through, unable to choose not to be sinful, and helpless even to desire of his or her own will to be other than sinful. Nor did he mean to discount the importance of the creation story. But he did start his famous TULIP theological system[1] with the letter *T*—*T* for "total depravity"—and Protestants ever since have tended to begin their account of the Good News with the disconcerting assertion that unregenerate men and women are dirty rotten sinners on their way to a fiery hell and unable to do anything about it.

It's hard to fault anyone for bailing out right there, thinking, as many are bound to do, *If that's the Good News, I don't even want to know what the Bad News is!*

Truthfully, I don't have any problem with Calvin's *T*, per se. There's ample evidence to support it in my neighborhood, and more from around the world every day in the news. I just think his theological system starts too late, essentially ignoring the foundational value of the creation story.

That beginning to the Great Story, and all that happens in the garden before the Fall, is too precious to relegate it to the status of a meaningless introduction. God's eager pleasure as he speaks different aspects of the cosmos into being, his tenderness as he forms man from earth and then woman from man, reminds me that the reason he wants to recover the wreck of this world and most especially the malevolent, mutant idiocy of humanity is, in part, because he remembers delighting in us the way we were. Fresh, new, squeaky clean, and full of perfect life.

The inference that he found it all so very good that he was in the habit of going for a late afternoon stroll around the grounds with Adam and Eve[2] is so sweetly evocative that it fills me with the hope that he just might consider it a pleasure to hang out with me too.

✠

Caleb was only five years old when his brand-new baby brother Kelly came home from the hospital. A week later, a crew of four or five of my construction mates pulled up in front of our two-bedroom bungalow and unloaded their tools. By noon that day, we had cut half of the roof off and built a new floor in its place.

Not much redevelopment had yet taken place in that neighborhood, and curiosity abounded. One rumor that came back to us was that our roof had been leaking and that was why we had removed the whole thing, leaving the house looking more like a bunker than a dwelling place. The story changed when the upper walls went up, and a rough, temporary exterior staircase sprouted from the front lawn to a newly framed second-story window. Now, apparently, those crazy people at 403 were building some kind of duplex apartment with its own separate entrance.

The truth was that, with two bedrooms and a fourth child, something had to give. Property values were such that it would cost all we could afford just to move. My own skills as a carpenter, plus access to cut rates for materials and other trades, made adding a second floor the way to go. In the course of time, the postwar brick cube took on the look of the century-old homes it was then my business to renovate, complete with dormered second-story windows, board and batten siding, and a wide front porch.

Nobody was more fascinated with the process than Caleb. By the time his birthday rolled around a few months later, the outer shell was secure: exterior walls up, windows in, and the roof complete.

Caleb's sixth birthday present was a hammer—a sixteen-ounce steel-shafted Stanley, with straight claws and a rubber grip. It was an adult hammer, not a toy, although several ounces lighter than my smallest hammer. With it came a holster, a steel ring mounted in a leather belt loop.

Caleb's eyes popped and his sober little face split in a wide grin when he opened the box. He babbled delightedly, swinging the hammer with abandon (I moved him carefully to the center of the room), sought assurance from me that it was, in fact, a "big person's hammer," then ran off to find a belt. When we got it all sorted out, he dropped the hammer through the steel ring as he had so often seen me do. The butt of the handle hung well below his knee. He looked up at me with an expression of sheer bliss.

It was the best dollar-to-delight ratio I've ever managed in a gift.

Although the outer shell of the addition was complete, there was still a lot of work to be done inside—the framing of interior walls, plumbing, heating and electrical, insulation, drywall, doors, trim, floor finishes, and a thousand other dusty details. I left the new upper floor sealed off from the original house, continuing to access the addition by the goofy looking stairway in the front yard.

The job went slowly, since I could only work on it when not engaged in my paying work or with family or church activities. Frankly, after the first several months, it was difficult to stay motivated. It helped that, from time to time, Caleb climbed up the stairs and through the window with me, to "help Dad build the house."

He prowled every corner of the room he would soon share with his brother Jesse, just four years old and too little to climb the stairs. He borrowed my tape measure so regularly that I found an old one he could keep for himself. But my little boy got bored just poking around, and wanted to do something to help. He wanted to work. He wanted to use that hammer.

So I got into the habit of giving him a handful of three-and-a-half-inch spikes and a pile of lumber cut-offs. That's a lot of nail for a six-year-old boy to drive home. Many adults who aren't used to swinging a hammer will take a dozen or more strokes, often glancing off the side of the nail and bending it or missing the head entirely.

I showed him how to set the nail, holding it well below the head with one hand and tapping it gently with the hammer until it would stand up on its own. Caleb had to hold the hammer with his little fist around the shaft just beneath the head in order to do it, but it didn't take long before he didn't need my help or instruction. As I worked elsewhere, I could hear the incessant tap-tap-tap-tap of him "working." He swung the hammer with two hands at first, slowly learning to let the weight of the tool do the work, and before long he was swinging it with one, lengthening his grip on the shaft as he became more confident.

There was no drywall up at the time, just bare stud walls, so we could see each other and converse the length of the house even when we were working in different rooms. Still, I often got absorbed in what I was doing and would lose track of him for long stretches of time. Caleb was never a kid who demanded a lot of attention.

Every now and then, after Caleb had "finished for the day," I'd be carrying a stack of two-by-fours from one room to another, or down the hallway, and come across a pile of lumber cut-offs. Without thinking about it, I'd try to swipe them out of the way with my boot—and discover that they were nailed to the floor. With three-and-a-half-inch spikes.

I'd pry the wood bits off the floor and bang the nails back out of them, or bend the points over. It cost me a few minutes each time and, since I kept forgetting, the odd sore toe from booting nailed-down lumber, but I never asked Caleb to stop.

Caleb's efforts weren't very productive. The truth is, his "help" cost me much more time and energy—both in coaching him how to hold the hammer, set the nail and so on, and in prying the pieces of lumber off the floor, removing or bending the nails so they wouldn't hurt anybody—than it should have been worth. But I still remember watching his earnest little face, completely absorbed in bringing that heavy hammer head down accurately, and with force, on the head of the nail; and listening to the tap of his hammer, or the studiously casual, proud way he would later describe to people how he was helping Dad build the house. The pleasure of sharing these things with my beloved son has never left me.

Because really, in some manner much more material than mere wood and nails, he *did* help me build the house.

God doesn't *need* my help. Not if he's even a fraction of the God I believe him to be. The one who speaks galaxies into being, creates the millions of creatures and billions of plants on this planet, all in a system that is self-sustaining, not to mention endlessly beautiful, then "needs" the help of Adam to look after it?

I don't think so.

The fact of the matter is that God could do far better without interference from man, whether it's the world's ecology or announcing the Good News that's in view. If I take it down another notch and apply this to my own situation, I have to admit that a God concerned with efficiency would not leave me in my role at Sanctuary.

I get in the way, fall asleep at the switch, am incapable of maintaining a true perspective, understand and communicate his Word poorly, and often just plain don't care very much. It's evident that God could do anything and everything much more easily without people like me around to clutter things up. So why doesn't he?

When the God-Who-Is-Three says to each other, *Let's make them in our image, then we'll let them rule over all the other stuff—fish, animals, birds, the earth itself,* I hear the delighted tones of one parent saying to the other, "Oh, let's let her try. How else is she going to learn? She's going to have so much fun with this!" My own "little story" experience with Caleb reminds me that the Great Story of God's pleasure is not so far-fetched.

It's not like Adam and Eve had a lot of game and resource management on their resumes. His pleasure in their participation is the only reason that makes sense.

Imagine God's pleasure when Adam woke up, and there beside him was the most gorgeous thing he had ever seen. Better than the rivers and waterfalls, more beautiful than the night sky brilliant with young stars, richer than any sunset. More cuddly somehow, despite the lack of fur, than even the cuddliest of the animals . . .

It wouldn't have hurt matters that she was naked.

The two of them standing there, unconsciously fabulous, thrilled speechless with each other. (Adam, anyway.) Touching, sniffing, inspecting each other all over, and eventually learning to do much more. God, there in the background, watching the whole thing. Pleased beyond words. Delighted with their shape, the texture of their skin, the softness of their hair, and most of all, their sweet intoxication with each other.

Imagine God bringing the animals to them, chuckling to

himself, *Right then, let's see what the kids do with this one: great flapping ears, silly grey skin three sizes too big even for it, and a nose that's so long it drags on the ground . . . It's a monster, a walking joke!*

I'm so glad the story starts here, and not with my ruin through Adam and Eve's fascination with fruit and knowledge. In it I hear my Father say that, although he needs nothing from me, he wants everything for me. He's not interested in squeezing the last drop out of me, or using me as some kind of tool he can pick up and put down as needed. He delights in having me hang out with him—strolling around the garden in the cool of the day.

He doesn't care that I spend most of my time nailing useless bits of wood to the floor, or that he'll have to fix my mess later. He doesn't snicker at my innocent delusion that I am doing Really Important Things. When I do become aware of my own insufficiency—when the hammer is too heavy for me and slips off the nail—he does not sniff and say, *You are a broken and pathetic thing, but I might choose to fix you anyway.*

His arm is around me, his hand supporting mine on the shaft of the wayward hammer, and I do not sense frustration, disappointment, or anger. I can hear a smile and the quiet delight in his voice.

> *Isn't this wonderful, my love? I'm so pleased that we're doing this together—you're helping me build the house!*

Part Three

THE FALL

SEVEN

THE BEAUTY OF A BROKEN MIRROR

My Child:

"I reared children and brought them up,
    but they have rebelled against me.
The ox knows his master,
    the donkey his owner's manger,
    but Israel does not know,
    my people do not understand."
Ah, sinful nation,
    a people loaded with guilt,
    a brood of evildoers,
    children given to corruption!
They have forsaken the LORD;
    they have spurned the Holy One of Israel
    and turned their backs on him.

Why should you be beaten anymore?
Why do you persist in rebellion?
Your whole head is injured,
    your whole heart afflicted.
From the sole of your foot to the top of
    your head there is no soundness—only
    wounds and welts and open sores,
    not cleansed or bandaged or soothed
    with oil . . .

"Come now, and let us reason together,"
Says the LORD,
"Though your sins are like scarlet,
They shall be as white as snow;
Though they are red as crimson,
They shall be like wool . . ."

—FROM ISAIAH, CHAPTER 1

These are not the words of an angry judge, distant and cold in condemnation. This is the sound of a loving and agonized parent, his soul torn by his child's rejection, his heart battered by the sight of the damage already done to his precious little one. Pleading with her to stop, to stop subjecting herself to such abuse. This is a wail of fear that worse is yet to come.

✠

She had flown more that two thousand miles to perform the most fruitless, pain-filled task I can imagine.

She came to bury her son.

Mrs. Flynn was possessed of that "old world" sort of gentility that made her feel shamefully underdressed if she went out in public without earrings and a row of pearls around her neck. She had flawless translucent skin, lovely silver hair, and a backbone of spring steel.

People die far too regularly in my community, and usually, like Mrs. Flynn's son Chris, too young and in unpleasant circumstances. More often than not, the family members who come to retrieve or lay to rest the remains of their wayward daughters and sons do so as expeditiously as possible. They're not usually eager to look too closely at the recent circumstances or lifestyle of the one who has passed, and even less so to meet their street brothers and sisters.

It's hard to fault them. I can only imagine the kind of pain some of my friends have caused their family members in the past; their present hardly bears looking at. Chris was no exception.

In his early forties when he died, Chris had been a raging alcoholic for years. Before that, a heroin addict—booze became his "cure" for the monkey on his back. He lived on the street or in hostels most of the time I knew him.

Despite all of that, Chris was a very, very bright man. He

claimed to have earned two university degrees, and although such claims in our community are often to be taken with a grain of salt, he certainly exhibited the requisite intellect. He was a storehouse of arcane information and wild but intriguing theories.

I can remember him gesticulating expansively and proclaiming, "We have to decentralize poverty!" and flapping his hands outward to demonstrate where poverty needed to go. "The suburbs don't take any responsibility for urban poverty! Their poor people keep migrating to the urban core because there are no programs to keep them in their communities of origin, and since they keep leaving, middle-class suburbanites and their leaders keep believing there is no poverty in their neighborhoods. Suburban leaders will only take responsibility for their own poor if those people start migrating back to the places they left, camping in their parks, panhandling on their streets! We have to decentralize poverty!"[1]

He actually talked like that, even when he was a little bit drunk, as he was that particular day. Sometimes he'd try to speak the street argot, but although he knew all the slang terms, they never sounded genuine in his mouth. He knew something about most things and had an opinion, loudly expressed, about everything. It was easy to dismiss Chris as little more than a mouthpiece, unless you spent time thinking about the ideas he presented or researched the facts he spouted incessantly.

At the memorial, the staff doctor at the hostel where Chris spent his last days told me, with a bemused expression on his face, that Chris had informed him that a particular medication he'd prescribed wouldn't work.

"Why not?" the doctor had asked.

"Because I drink," Chris responded kindly, patting the doctor's knee.

"I don't think that will matter much," the doctor said.

"Oh yes it will." Chris went on to describe in detail how the liver functions, and why the alcohol to which he was addicted would counteract the specific meds the doctor was recommending.

The doctor was so impressed by Chris's accurate explanation of liver biophysics that he researched the properties of the medicine he had prescribed. Chris was right. A liver already busy processing alcohol would simply flush it out.

Mrs. Flynn brought pictures. There was one of Chris in a bathtub with a couple of other children, his beaming, cherubic face recognizable to me even after forty years and a lot of very rough road. Another of him in his early twenties, before the addictions overwhelmed him, wearing the large plastic-rimmed eyeglasses that were fashionable in the late seventies. My heart gave a lurch when I saw them. Chris had been dubbed "Goggles" on the street because of his penchant for outlandish eyewear.

As she showed me the photographs, Mrs. Flynn spoke quietly about what a bright, happy little boy her Chris had been. How well he had done in high school, and then in university—yes, two degrees. She had nothing to say about Mr. Flynn, except that he had died years earlier and that she and Chris, then in his teens, had moved west immediately afterward. I thought her reticence about her husband, and the fact that she did not wonder aloud what had gone wrong with Chris, quite telling, but I asked no questions.

Mrs. Flynn attended the memorial at Sanctuary. We displayed poster-board copies of the pictures. She met Chris's street friends, and though many of them were rough, unsteady on their feet, and smelled of liquor, she shook their hands and listened to them pour out grief-stricken and often wholly inappropriate tales of their adventures with her son, with the stately gravity of royalty.

In private, she told me that she had an interview with a police officer who was investigating Chris's death. He had died in his sleep at the hostel, but the hostel records reported that he had been badly beaten a couple of weeks earlier and had been sluggish and disoriented ever since. If the officer was able to find out who had beaten Chris, it was possible that murder charges would be filed.

It was entirely plausible. Although Chris, like many homeless men, often postured as if he was a tough guy, he was hopeless with his fists and unable to control his mouth. I knew that his know-it-all attitude and innate ability to make his peers feel intellectually inferior had led to his becoming a human punching bag in the previous couple of years.

I could see that Mrs. Flynn understood this. Despite her calm, dignified exterior, it was clear that her mother's heart was enduring a beating to rival the ones Chris had taken. By the time we stood side by side in the cemetery, just the two of us and a niece, her beautiful skin had become like crumpled tissue paper. I wondered at the grace she had displayed earlier at the

Sanctuary memorial, taking in her delicate hands fist after swollen fist, many with split knuckles, and knowing all the time any one of them might have been the end of her boy.

She had foreseen the end decades earlier, had grieved it all that time, had suffered from a distance the knowledge of her son's suffering and humiliation. And now, impossibly, the end was here already. Her brilliant, shining young Chris, rendered to ash.

A final prayer; the urn disappearing into a narrow hole in the hungry earth.

When I listen intently to the conversation between God and Adam and Eve, after they have eaten the forbidden fruit,[2] I can hear echoes of a hundred such conversations I had as a child with my own parents, and as a parent with my children. God, as parents do, begins asking uncomfortable questions . . .

Where are you? Why are you hiding from me? What's wrong between us? Who told you that you were naked? Have you done what I warned you not to do? Oh, no . . . What have you done?

I can hear in his voice the dismay of a parent whose child has for the first time consciously chosen to reject the parent's love to selfishly pursue a thrillingly independent but dangerous course. The dread, the awful sinking realization that this choice has changed things forever, that there is no turning back, and that it will all get much, much worse before—if ever—it gets better.

In the craven, finger-pointing words of Eve, and especially of Adam, I recognize my own wheedling tone when my childish ego has pulled the house down upon me, and I am desperate to escape responsibility for the destruction.

"It wasn't me! It was her! She practically forced me to eat it! And you gave her to me, so really, it's your fault!"

"I didn't know what I was doing—the devil made me do it!"

What they have to say in their defense is so transparently lame that God doesn't even bother to argue it with them. Instead, he explains to them—and with sorrow, I'm convinced, rather than anger—the curse that will befall them as the inevitable result of the choice they have made. Already it has changed the nature of the relationship between Adam and Eve forever. Will she ever forget how quickly and completely Adam distanced himself from her—who the day before had been his greatest delight—and laid every fault he could at her door? Will he, unwilling to accept responsibility for his own failure, ever stop resenting her for having persuaded him to eat the fruit?

The expression of "the Curse," if you consider the endless historical ramifications of it, is remarkably concise. God doesn't go on and on, lambasting them for their foolishness and asking, *How could you do this to me after all I've done for you?* Listening carefully, I can hear behind God's dignified restraint his deep, deep sigh. *This is not the way I wanted it to be for you . . .*

I need to remember this. That pain and sorrow and endless exhausting toil were not in his plan. That the domination of women, or anyone for that matter, is a result, not an unceasing punishment.

God knows how inexorably humanity will gravitate toward evil and how quickly that evil compounds itself, perverting its host. The God-Who-Is-Three discusses the matter and agrees that the death Adam and Eve had been warned of must take place. Yet even here, as in the earlier promise of the coming One who will crush the serpent's head, there is a whisper of grace.

So, too, the agonized lament of the Father recorded by Isaiah. Out of the epic story of Yahweh's relationship with the nation of Israel, I can hear him groaning to me, in those many private places where I bleed:

Oh, look at you! Battered and bruised almost beyond recognition. Suppurating wounds that you don't even know enough to cleanse and bandage.

I never raised you to this! Don't you see that it's the result of your rebellion? It's completely unnecessary for you to keep on being beaten. You're so sick you can't even tell how ill you really are.

Come, talk about it with me. Let me bind your scarlet wounds with fresh linen, white as snow . . .[3]

The story of his agelong fidelity to the people of Israel tells me that the Father has not abandoned me, his child, either. He never will. My sin is the proving ground of his grace. Every brutal, sordid aspect of humanity's brokenness, every war, every rape, every dark corner of my own self-absorbed heart, and every secret, venal, destructive thought or action emanating from it is a testament to my Father's determination to stick with me. Despite the agony it causes him.

The Fall, and my own willful disobedience, has broken the image of my Father in me, like a mirror shattered into a thousand shards. Yet each jagged piece still in some small way reflects an aspect of his being, and he will not dispose of it. The Fall is not the utter ruin of my relationship with him, but the proof of its ultimate inviolability. He is not sweeping those shards into a dusty pile to be thrown into the trash, cursing the inconvenience. He is gathering them, every sparkling sliver. Assembling them into a new mosaic of his identity uniquely reflected in mine.

My brokenness cuts him. The proof of his fidelity:
bright beads of blood on his fingers.

EIGHT

DREAMING OF ME

My Love:

God has poured out his love into our hearts by the
Holy Spirit, whom he has given us. You see, at just
the right time, when we were still powerless, Christ
died for the ungodly . . . God demonstrates his own
love for us in this: While we were still sinners, Christ
died for us.

—FROM PAUL'S LETTER TO THE ROMANS,
CHAPTER 5

Places where sacrifices have been made are holy places. All my life I have been "brought to the cross" so that a tepid version of it, sanitized by art and comfortable church sanctuaries, has long since become a familiar, safe place for me. But standing here on a dusty road, jostled by outbound pilgrims eager to get home and local farmers carrying their produce to market, it's hard to see the sanctity of it. Three short, mean little crosses, planted so close to the road that passersby can spit on the groaning figures nailed to them without breaking stride. They don't even know who the criminals are; most can't even read the satirical title nailed, along with its defendant, to the cross in the middle.

There is no serene, back-lit hill here. The crosses are not majestically distant. There is only a ghastly lump of rock behind them, its rough domed shape and a couple of shallow caves like empty eye sockets providing a macabre backdrop. A couple of bored soldiers gambling in the background.

If I dare to stand close enough to the middle cross and can filter out the rough jokes and catcalls of the commuters, I can hear him breathing. Gasping. He is in constant, increasingly feeble motion, rising on pierced feet to take the weight off his hands and to relieve the crushing pressure on his lungs and heart. His breathing eases a little then, but he begins to sag again almost as soon as he has pushed himself up straight.

This is love?

Every fresh group on the road behind me passes with a wave of muttered disgust. It doesn't bear looking at, but I do seek out his face. Isaiah was right: "There were many who were appalled at him—his appearance was so disfigured beyond that of any man . . . He had no beauty or majesty to attract us to him, nothing in his appearance that we should desire him. He was despised and rejected . . ."[1]

I can't stand to stay here for long, not if I really look and listen. It's dirty, gory, sordid. His every breath a wrenching moan. I need to find some safer, more mundane way to witness the embodiment of this word *love*.

✠

There are also, in our Sanctuary neighborhood, holy places that look like anything but. One such is the deep concrete well of a stairway to a nearby underground parking garage. Steel handrails coated long ago with a pale blue paint, now chipped and pitted, worn to bare metal at each landing where people grab them and swing themselves around, plummet past the exit doors at each successive parking level.

The floor at the very bottom, perhaps six or seven feet square, is invariably strewn with old newspapers, dirty syringes, and the wrinkled husks of used condoms. An upward look reveals a square of distant sky that seems, from there, always to be the same lifeless grey as the steps and walls.

One bitter night near the end of February, Seven and Lila slipped away from an evening meal at Sanctuary and scampered across Yonge Street to the stairwell. Clutched in one of Seven's fists was a few minutes of relief from the grinding harshness of homelessness in winter, but they didn't get to use it.

They found Rob sprawled on the floor at the bottom of the stairwell, motionless, swollen, and already turning blue. That seems like a euphemism until you actually see it: purple lips and deadly pale skin, tinted at each hollow of cheek and eye the color of very old denim.

Lila ran back to Sanctuary to collect Keren and Doug, members of the Sanctuary staff. They returned with her to await the arrival of the paramedics, and to support Seven as he made his statement to the police. The paramedics were still trying to resuscitate Rob as they were removing him from the stairwell, but by the time they arrived at the hospital, he still had a body temperature of thirty degrees Celsius[2] and no vital signs. He was in his forties, but looked much older, of course—a First Nations man with a rough, deeply pocked complexion and a long gray ponytail. He might have been handsome once, but there was nothing attractive about him now. His crutches were found at the top of the stairwell. A quiet, solitary sort, Doug had connected with him pretty regularly on the street. Rob had recently told him he'd had enough and was ready to go.

Somebody had mentioned to Keren a few days before that heroin was being peddled in our immediate neighborhood again. It had been mostly crack and crystal meth for years. It's one thing to do those drugs in the bitter cold—they keep you up and buzzing—but after years of uppers to bang a downer like heroin . . . She wondered if Rob had gone on the nod, as people do with smack, drifting off to sleep despite being in the ice box of an open concrete stairwell in freezing temperatures.

It wasn't unusual to find that Rob had a wife and kid he had long ago left behind. It *was* unusual that they wanted to make the six-hour drive south to Toronto to bury him with dignity in the Cree tradition. The elder who led the ceremony hadn't known Rob and so confined himself to drumming, offering the spirit plate to unseen guests, inviting visible guests to smudge,[3] and singing to the four directions of the medicine wheel.

Knowing already that Rob had long been separated from them by his drug and alcohol use, it came as a further surprise when his ex-wife and son chose to speak about him directly, and with great dignity and compassion.

The son—a lean, smoldering kid in his teens—talked about how his father had only been able to speak to him when he was drinking. It had bothered the son so much that only then could Rob express his feelings, that the boy had stopped making the trek to the city to seek his father out. But his father had always told him to be strong, and he *would* be strong, and . . . The boy faltered, his brave lip quivering, and sat down.

His mother embraced him briefly and moved to the lectern. She thanked the small group that had gathered for coming and for their care of Rob through the years. Nobody we knew on the street was close to Rob; not surprisingly, none of our street friends had come to the funeral service. The handful in attendance were social workers and ministers.

The one intimate bit of information any of us was able to offer was Rob's standing joke, his street alias. He'd retained his real first name, but if asked to identify himself, he'd say, "My name's Rob. Rob Banks." And he'd show his teeth in a grim little smile.

His wife's words stunned me with their grace, considering the pain he'd caused, and that he had abandoned wife and child some fifteen years earlier.

"Rob was a man of great courage and generosity," she began. She went on to describe how, when their son was only two years old, Rob had told her that he was leaving. He explained he could see that his addictions were harming her and the boy; he was unable to defeat them and couldn't live with the damage he was doing to the ones he loved. He would go and, by going, grant her and his son freedom to live their lives in health and dignity.

And so he disappeared into the desert canyons of the city's streets and dark alleys, its glass-and-steel wilderness and stair-well caves.

My cynical soul would have concluded that he had only given a noble name to selfish weakness, but she went on to say that he had called her regularly through all those years, to see how the boy was doing and to tell her he still loved them both. He sent money when he could—not much, but then an addict who panhandles to get by rarely has a ready store of cash. She said she had told him he should come home a few times, but he had always refused—not, he said, until he was no longer addicted, and could be sure he would hurt them no more.

I wondered, then, at the sacrifice he had made. At the

peculiar strength at the heart of his abject weakness. I wondered if he had left his crutches at the top of the long descent because he had no intention of climbing back up. I thought of him lying on the icy floor staring at the puny cube of sky above him, dreaming of the life his son might have.

The eternal night, falling, falling.

✠

The sacrifice God made by turning Adam and Eve out of the garden of Eden is astonishing enough to me. No more would he be able to delight in daily intimacy with the two he loved so much; no more ambling through the trees and beside the rivers, watching the animals play while chatting contentedly with the two beautiful young lovers. He had created everything for precisely this purpose, and now, to avoid the horror of their bodies continuing forever while their souls crumbled into a grotesque parody of the image in which they had been created, he would have to watch them leave.

He would have to take a voluntary step back, allowing them to face the consequences of their actions with only the memory of his love—and the knowledge that he was watching over them from afar—to protect them.

This is a costly kind of love. Knowing that to truly save them it would take the destruction of the world as they knew it—the world he had so lovingly crafted for them—and thousands of generations of alienation and suffering while he watched it all with an anguished heart.

But the sacrifice of the cross, the costliness of that kind of love, is of a whole other order. It's daunting even to look at it, let alone get close enough to hear his agonized breathing. This is not what I want love to look like.

Here, I can understand why Paul referred to the "offense of the cross."[4] It's gruesome. Fresh blood oozing over the brownish dried stuff from the first beating. It's not surprising to me that many dismiss this part of the story as bloodthirstiness, or quibble about how, really, can this atonement business work? In our sanitized middle-class western lives, there isn't much space for a scene as raw as this.

The cross terrifies me. Against every natural desire, if I dare get close enough, I recognize in this unrecognizable, mutilated, and humiliated form the image of the wreck of humanity, the horror of what Adam and Eve, once beautiful in their innocence, have become. Worse: I recognize my own helpless, ugly, utterly fallen self. The darkest, most unlovely, perverse, wicked aspects of what I fear myself to be. This is the self I am desperate to keep hidden from everyone; even, as much as possible, from myself.

Standing here, I cannot escape it. If the Son stood in the Jordan for me, and received the blessing from above for me, he hangs on this cross for me also. Stretched, like me, between earth and sky, receiving every judgment that ever was due me.

I have feared to be so truly known by anyone, convinced that the darkest truths of my soul would be as appalling as the face of the one who hangs on the cross. But because he has seen his Son thus, allowed him to become thus, I know the Father can see me also at my most degraded, and love me still.

Golgotha is, ultimately, the end of every form of sin and death. Its power reaches backward and forward in history, encompasses the universe, defeats all darkness. But because God is God, it is also directly and intimately personal. Paul speaks the language of my longing heart when he says that his old, bruised, and broken self died there with Jesus; that he is now living a new kind of life, animated by trusting that the Son of God "loved *me* and gave himself for *me*."[5]

Trusting this myself, I can creep toward the squalid killing ground at the base of that eerie rock. Holy ground. He is sprawled on the timbers, and the soldiers are stretching out his arms and feet. His chest heaves in agitation, but he makes no sound. A hammer, raised.

As it falls, he is gazing upward, dreaming of me.

NINE

CHOCOLATE ROSEBUDS

My Pleasure:

There were shepherds living out in the fields nearby, keeping watch over their flocks at night. An angel of the Lord appeared to them . . . the angel said to them, "Do not be afraid. I bring you good tidings of great joy that will be for all the people. Today in the town of David a Savior has been born to you; he is Christ the Lord. This will be a sign to you: You will find a baby wrapped in cloths and lying in a manger."

Suddenly a great company of the heavenly host appeared with the angel, praising God and saying, "Glory to God in the highest, and on earth peace to men on whom his favor rests."

—FROM THE GOSPEL OF LUKE, CHAPTER 2

> The Spirit of the Sovereign LORD is on me,
> because the LORD has anointed me
> to preach good news to the poor.
> He has sent me to bind up the brokenhearted,
> to proclaim freedom for the captives
> and release from darkness for the prison-
> ers, to proclaim the year of the LORD's
> favor . . .

—FROM ISAIAH, CHAPTER 61 (THE GOSPEL OF LUKE, CHAPTER 4)

As God's fellow workers we urge you not to receive God's grace in vain. For he says, "In the time of my favor I heard you, and in the day of salvation I helped you."

I tell you, *now* is the time of God's favor, *now* is the day of salvation.

—FROM 2 CORINTHIANS, CHAPTER 6, EMPHASIS ADDED

Although I may have a tough time really believing it, I get why God calls me his child. He made me, after all. Even writers of lousy poetry and painters of crummy paintings are often proud of their work.

I sort of get why he says he loves me, too—God is love, after all, so he pretty much has to, doesn't he? Couldn't do otherwise.

But when he says, *I'm pleased with you*, it really stumps me.

I mean, really, the God who has entire galaxies to play with just can't wait to hang out with me? It's hard enough to believe while still in the garden, where, at least, the surroundings are pleasant, and his image in me is still so bright and shiny. But out here in the desert, where the unforgiving light reveals me as being unsound from head to foot, a walking compendium of wounds and bruises and gangrenous sores, it seems absurd.

In this state, why would he want to get close to me? What pleasure could I possibly bring him?

When I was very small, shorter than the kitchen countertop, I reached way up to take a piece of the apple my mother had cut into slices a few moments before, and grabbed instead the knife she had used. It sliced the tip from the middle finger of my left hand.

Bundling the dangling bit of flesh back onto the finger and me into the car, she drove me to the doctor's office, where he sewed it back on. There's a lump on that finger to this day, and a tiny crease down the center of it, as if that digit wears a minute bum of its own.

I'm not sure if I actually remember the event itself or merely myself telling my mother what I remembered when I got to be eight or nine. I know she was surprised that by then I remembered it at all. But here's the curious thing: I didn't remember any pain or blood, my mother's upset, or the drive to the doctor.

I remembered the stitches, before the ends were clipped, standing up from the end of my finger as if it had suddenly grown hair. And I remembered my mother stopping at a drugstore on the way home and buying me a box of chocolate rosebuds.

✠

It seems no small miracle to me that my four children were all born without handicaps and have grown to young adulthood without suffering any serious, permanent damage. In fact, as I contemplated trying to express in this chapter the many ways God has breathed the Great Story of his favor toward humanity into my small life story, I thought often of a number of my friends who have lost their children to accident or illness, or whose precious little ones were born with serious handicaps.

The privilege of walking, during a few important moments, beside my friends Doug and Val as they faced the searing agony of losing their beautiful daughter Alison, impacted me deeply. I can hardly write about it, even this briefly and more than a dozen years later, without tears.

The matter-of-fact love and faithfulness of my lifelong pals

Heather Ann and Doug toward their adult daughter Jocelyn, who has Prader-Willi Syndrome, are similarly inspiring. The complexity of the challenges they face together is enormous, the frustrations continual, but they carry on with a delightful humor that makes them a joy to be with.

But ultimately it's my own children, with their very "normal" mishaps and situations, who have spoken most intimately into my life—simply because they're mine. The trials we have faced together are not of the cataclysmic sort endured by the friends I have mentioned, but God does speak through them.

Jesse is the kamikaze of the family, the Champion of Broken and Dislocated Bones (although lately, his sister Rachel has been closing the gap). Eager to move from the moment of his birth, Jesse never has had a good sense of safe physical limits. At eleven months of age, only a month or so after he had begun to walk, I entered the living room one day to find him standing on top of my old upright piano. His face beaming, he waved his hands in the air as he wobbled to and fro, ready to dive from the narrow top.

At three or four, with his older brother Caleb urging him on ("Go higher, Jesse! Go higher!"), he climbed the corkscrew willow tree in the backyard. At his mother's command to "Come down from there!" he did, leaping from the high branch he'd been standing on, pinballing off the lower branches on his way down until he landed in a heap on the ground. Scraped and bruised, but still smiling. Caleb explained later that he had been hoping Jesse would get stuck, and that firemen and a fire truck would have to come remove him from the tree.

He has broken his wrist snowboarding, an ankle twice, the first time while jumping a flight of stairs, dislocated the same poor joint playing rugby, endured surgery on a shoulder dislocated in the course of a hockey game and repeatedly thereafter, and more. Most, if not all of Jesse's injuries have occurred because he goes just a little farther, risks just a little bit more than most people.

My youngest son, Kelly, on the other hand, is the Prince of Undeserved Calamity.

☩

The door swung open, and a doctor I had seen once or twice before entered, followed by a clutch of residents and interns I had not. Having been through this a few times already and knowing what was coming, I got up from the chair I had been sitting in and laid Kelly gently on the bed. He was dopey and radiating heat like a little furnace, but not complaining. He never does.

The lead doctor had been explaining Kawasaki Syndrome as he came through the door, telling his acolytes that it was an acute febrile illness of unknown etiology, an inflammation of blood vessels and so manifesting itself throughout the whole body. Quite rare in North America—only 850 documented cases, ever![1] Consequently, almost always misdiagnosed early on as an ear infection or scarlet fever. Afflicting only boys, usually five years of age or under. Danger of aneurysms in the heart itself. These not generally lethal to the patient at first presentation since young hearts are so flexible, but with the potential of later complications, especially in the absence of good, early treatment—arrhythmia, infarction, of course . . .

Warming to his subject, the doctor gently picked up one of Kelly's feet and then a limp hand, displaying to his audience the cherry red color of sole and palm. They looked as if they had been placed on an ink pad. The heat of his blood was burning the skin off his extremities.

"This is great. We love seeing this," the doctor enthused as he moved upward to point out the bright lips and glowing inner ears of my son.

"Excuse me," I interrupted. None of the earlier stuff had bothered me much, since I had heard it all before, but this was going a little too far. The doctor looked at me directly for the first time, and in mild surprise.

"Some of us," I said, "don't think this is so great. Some of us are not so pleased to see it."

Embarrassed, the doctor harrumphed that, of course, it wasn't good that, ah, my son had this disease or was in discomfort, but that, uh, he had just meant to point out that, since the disease is generally not accurately diagnosed for five or six days, this was, um, a rare opportunity to see the symptoms in, ah, full blush. He waved an explanatory hand at the group behind him, who had been craning forward with great interest only a minute ago, and now stood with blank expressions and clipboards raised protectively against their chests.

"I've never seen the symptoms this early or this clearly myself!" he said brightly.

"I know," I responded. Hitching my chair closer to the bed, putting a hand on Kelly's hot little arm. "But this is my son."

☩

It turned out later that Kelly did have an aneurysm in his heart. Ten years of regular follow-up testing ultimately revealed that, thankfully, his heart had fully repaired itself.

The summer before, when he was only four, he had an anaphylactic reaction to the sting of a yellowjacket, a kind of wasp. His nasal passages swelled shut in minutes, but his throat stayed open. A two-year course of painful injections built up his immunities so that he can embark on the canoe trips he now loves without fearing that a small bug might end his life.

The winter following his encounter with Kawasaki Syndrome, Kelly was walking home from school with his sister, Rachel. A garbage truck suddenly pulled into a driveway in front of them. The children stopped, but Kelly slipped on some ice and the truck rolled to a stop on top of his foot. When I found him in the emergency room, he was sitting up on a gurney, pale but playing quietly with some toys. His crushed foot looked like a small football, mottled a sickening purple and black. The toes were rendered almost invisible by swelling. For years after, when he was tired or cold, I'd see him absently standing on one foot, the other raised to relieve the discomfort. But he's fine now. He plays hockey, and cycles, and works every day as a carpenter. The foot is completely healed.

I could go on about the tow rope that snapped under stress—while tubing behind a powerboat—and lashing back, struck him in the eye, blinding it completely for about a month one summer. His eyesight is far better than mine now, thanks—but I think you get the picture. You might expect Kelly to have a bleak outlook on life, but he doesn't. He laughs a lot and doesn't have a sullen or self-pitying bone in his body.

When I hear the angels announce that God's favor rests on me, and I wonder how this can be so in my broken, fallen state, I think of how my heart has been drawn to my sons when they have been hurting or ill. It's no coincidence that the announcement was made to express God's joy at the birth of his own Child.

Whether the pain my boys have endured has been, as has often been the case with Jesse, the result of their own risky actions, or, as with Kelly, the inexplicably random stuff that just happens through no fault of his own, my favor rests on them just the same. My reaction to their suffering, their illness or injury, isn't anger at their thoughtless behavior or disgust at their infirmity, but a deeper-than-ever desire to be near them. One way or another, once the immediate crisis has been faced, my instinctual reaction is not to complain to them about the cost or inconvenience of their ills, but to bless them—to give them chocolate rosebuds. Their crises serve to make me more aware than ever of just how much they mean to me.

I love to hear Jesus proclaim the year of the Lord's favor—the time when he looks with pleasure upon me, and others who are poor, brokenhearted, imprisoned by situations or habits, and unable to see clearly enough to make any real change. I love it because I hear him announce his intention to enact justice and grace for the very people whom everyone else has discarded. I hear him express himself in most personal terms as well: he takes no pleasure in my condition or situation, but his heart is drawn to me precisely because of it.

Maybe the mothers of Galilee used the wild stories about the pathetic figure on the Gentile side of the lake as a means of encouraging good behavior in their children. *If you don't eat your vegetables, the Demon Man of Gesara may come in the night and eat them for you—and take a bite of you as a side dish! He lives in a graveyard, he's filthy and always hungry, strong as an ox, a Gentile dog who howls at the moon and wears nothing but chains hanging from his ankles and wrists . . .*

Perhaps Jesus heard the lurid stories as he traveled the Nazareth-Capernaum circuit. Maybe he had always known about him. Whatever the case, it was the man's desperate state that drew him. It must have frustrated the disciples to hear the Master say, just as the crowds were beginning to really warm up to his teaching, "I want you to take me across the lake again, and land me right opposite the tombs where he lives." I can almost hear them grumbling about leaving the big opportunities behind to go visit one crazy reject as they step the sail.

The boat has barely grounded on the shore when the man appears from a gap in the rocks a couple of hundred feet away. He comes running toward them, stumbling and tumbling among the stones, gashing himself without seeming to notice. He's huge, a naked brute, a human nightmare of hair and scabs and flying spittle. Falling to his knees while still at a distance, he flings trembling hands in the air and begins to bawl his fear that this one, too, has come only to torment him. Like the villagers, the herdsmen, the gawkers from the Ten Cities who come in groups to view, from a safe distance, the freak who lives among the bones of the dead.

The one he fears steps from the boat and walks slowly toward him. The voices in the man's head are screaming from his mouth, screaming past what he wants to say, trying to drown out the quiet command of the Galilean to come out and leave the man alone. The Galilean ignores the insane babble.

"What is your name?" he asks suddenly, and the man knows the Galilean is speaking past the voices to him, to him. The voices are shocked to silence for the briefest moment, then they begin shrieking again, all at once.

"What is your name?" the Galilean asks again. He keeps asking the same question,[2] and as he does, the man who has been buried beneath the voices for longer than he can remember begins to rise.

Later, the man will hear the strange story of the stampeding suicidal pigs. But all he registers now is a frightening internal tumbling of himself among the voices, as if he was falling down a hill of large stones . . . except that he seems to be falling up . . .

He is not aware, either, that the herdsmen have gone running in panic to tell the owners of the pigs what has happened, or that word has spread through the village and across the countryside. He's not sure how he ended up this way, clothed somehow, sitting beside the Galilean with their backs against a warm rock and their faces toward the late afternoon sun. They are chatting quietly, and the only other voices to be heard are those of the Galilean's friends muttering amongst themselves on the shore by the boat.

Before long the mob appears, lathered in sweat and indignation. The handful at the front of the crowd, picking their way along the rocky shore as far from the tombs as possible, are already complaining loudly about the loss of the herd and demanding compensation. Their voices tumble over each other in a way that is painfully familiar to the man sitting beside the Galilean. Although the men by the boat seem unconcerned, as if they have seen this kind of thing before, the man begins to wonder if the crowd will turn nasty.

He is large, and strong. He shifts his weight a little, in case he needs to leap to his feet to defend the Galilean, and that's when one or two of the people closest to him look for the first time directly at him. The shock is plain on their faces when they realize who he is, and then the most peculiar thing: the shock is overtaken by fear. This is not the thrilling fear of his old tormentors, ready to heave rocks and insults at him before fleeing down the path to the village.

It's the Galilean himself who frightens them. Because he is sitting at his ease, watching the sun dance on the water, enjoying the companionship of the untamable Wild Man of Gesara. Unconcerned about the loss of the herd—one would think he thought it a good transaction, two thousand pigs for one demon-infested piece of human trash. The Galilean leans close to the man, to be heard above the crowd, which is pleading now rather than demanding that he leave their shores. The man can feel the breath on his neck as he speaks.[3]

✠

I would love to have been in on that conversation. I would love to have watched the two of them sitting together, enjoying the serene moments before the mob showed up. When I listen carefully, I can hear the kinds of things they must have said, and I realize that it must have been much like a conversation Jesus might have with me. I can hear him chuckle,

> I know you were a mess. Still are! Why do you think I made Peter and the boys sail me across the lake? It was your need, and your inability to do anything about it, that tugged at my heart. Look, you might think of yourself as a total screw-up—and let's be honest: in

a purely factual, empirical fashion, you're right—but you're my boy. None of that stuff defines you in my eyes, nor does the way others may label you. I want to be nowhere else so much as I want to be with you, right here between the wounds of your past and the challenges of your future.

You're welcome, he says, when I thank him for rescuing me, or for loving me in spite of my unloveliness. *It's my pleasure.*

Paul's words to the Corinthians confirm to me that I'm hearing him accurately. Just a few verses before the one quoted at the head of the chapter, he says that God views me as a "new creation"—that in his eyes, all the old, broken, fallen stuff that defined me is gone. God, by the death of Jesus, has reconciled the world to himself, and he is "not counting men's sins against them." Phew.

One way of saving something is by rescuing it from danger. Another is by keeping it safe. In either case, the saving is done because what has been saved is valuable to the one doing the saving—like my father's watch, which is precious to me even though the crystal is cracked and it has never kept time as well as the much cheaper one I wear every day.

My pleasure rests upon you, right here, right now, God is saying to me. *Not later, right now.*

> *I am so pleased with you that I am saving you,*
> *rescuing you, keeping you for myself.*

Part Four

REDEMPTION

TEN

STRIKING OFF THE CHAINS

My Child:

The Scripture declares that the whole world is a prisoner of sin, so that what was promised, being given through faith in Jesus Christ, might be given to those who believe. Before this faith came, we were held prisoners by the law, locked up until faith should be revealed . . .

You are all sons of God through faith in Christ Jesus, for all of you who were baptized into Christ have clothed yourselves with Christ. There is neither Jew nor Greek, slave nor free, male nor female, for you are all one in Christ . . .

Because you are sons, God sent the Spirit of his Son into our hearts, the Spirit who calls out, *"Abba*, Father."

So you are no longer a slave, but a son; and since you are
a son, God has made you also an heir.

—FROM GALATIANS, CHAPTERS 3 AND 4

We waited until Jesse had arrived, after completing the long drive from Ottawa to Toronto, before taking my father off life support. My mother had insisted that it be so, and I'm glad she did. Despite warnings from medical personnel that Dad might linger many hours, or even days, he was gone within ten minutes.

I'd been at the bedside of too many dying people before, including a few who were on life support, but when it's your father lying there . . . Still as death already but for the chest rising with such mechanical regularity, dropping sharply as the respirator pump clicks off, a motion so unnatural that it confers no illusion of life. When it's your father, it's hard to tell if time has stopped, or the world has gone spinning off its axis.

My father was the strongest, fittest seventy-nine-year-old man I have ever met. He watched what he ate, worked out several times each week—and that, ironically, was the death of him. One Thursday morning in May, he went as usual to the exercise room in the swanky condo where he lived with my mother. Going to a large, overhead television monitor, he turned it to face the machine he planned to use. When several other residents heard the story later, they turned pale and, after swallowing hard, told us, "I used to do exactly the same thing . . ."

The bracket holding the television snapped. The entire weight of the big CRT unit dropped onto my father's upturned head, fracturing his forehead and cheek, driving him backward to the floor. A compound fracture of his leg; more fractures at the back of his skull. He wasn't breathing when he was found. Paramedics estimated he had been almost half an hour without oxygen before they got him started up again.

He probably should have died there on the floor. It became quickly apparent that it was highly unlikely he'd ever regain consciousness, and that, even if he did, he would be severely brain damaged. Seventy-two hours of medical observation, seventy-two hours of vigil for my mother, my brother John and I, as well as other family members coming and going, made it plain that even that very slim possibility had dissipated. A doctor presented the options; the only realistic decision was made. I phoned Jesse to tell him it was time to come, and my brother Dave in England to suggest he hold off until we knew what would happen with the funeral.

Three generations of his family, entire but for Dave and his young son Keir, stood shoulder to shoulder around my father's bed. Our eyes streaming, chests constricted—but some disconnected part of the self distantly whispering, "This can't be real," into the blue half-light of the ICU. Dad's forehead and hands were swollen, his cheeks rough with three days' stubble, but his skin color was good, his hair still thick and black. No more pump-and-wheeze of the respirator. We had been brought back into the room immediately after it had been removed, and already his chest was barely moving—a hardly perceptible flutter every thirty seconds, every minute. Every two minutes . . .

Finally, the utter stillness. The stillness that mocks every other form of calm; the subtle but definite change in the tone and texture of skin.

┼

Every great story has a climax: that moment toward which every previous part of the story has been building, and upon which every subsequent development depends. It's the moment upon which the very nature of the story hangs. Will Frodo find the strength to throw the Ring into the Crack of Doom, or will he keep it and become a monster? Will MacBeth resist the temptations of ambition and do the noble thing, or succumbing, plant the seeds of his own destruction? Will young Dia hear the voice of his father and reclaim his true identity as a beloved son, or will he resist and disappear completely into his new persona as a soulless killing machine?[1]

Redemption is the climax of the Great Story. To *deem* is to have an opinion about something and, particularly, to render a judgment about it. I might, for example, deem a cause worthy of my support. To *re*deem, then, can be understood as rendering a new judgment about something that has previously been judged. To *re*name, to *re*define, to assign a new value or identity.

This is exactly what Solomon Vandy, an African fisherman in the movie *Blood Diamond*, does after passing through a human hell in an attempt to recover his son from the clutches of a self-described "devil" who has turned the boy into a drug-fueled child soldier. Finally holding the boy in his arms, but discovering that young Dia no longer recognizes him and instead curses and rejects him, Solomon redeems his son—he speaks over and over the truth about who Dia really is, the details of his character and identity, until the child hears and begins to accept it.

There is, however, a further value to the word *redemption*. It means "to buy something back which has been sold or lost, having recognized its inherent preciousness"; specifically, it means "to purchase one who has been sold into slavery, for the purpose of setting him or her free."

Paul's words to the Galatian Christians express the very climax of the Great Story. The idea of redemption has been foreshadowed in many places in the story before now. The children of Israel, a nation literally born into slavery, is "purchased" by God and set free; the Law subsequently delivered by Moses includes requirements and provisions for the redemption of livestock, real estate, and even people who may yet sell themselves into slavery.

Before all this, Job, the most ancient of biblical writers, has called upon the All-Sufficient One to redeem him out of his torment; has, in fact, named him as "my Redeemer."[2] For a thousand years after, prophets and poets proclaim the willingness and intention of Yahweh to redeem his people out of the disobedience, oppression, and affliction into which they so routinely fall. His agenda is justice—a return for the lost, broken, and enslaved to health, wholeness, and vital relationship with their tribe and their God.

Inherent in the idea of redemption is the concept that such freedom comes only at a price. That price, of course, is the very life of the Son of God. The *moment* of redemption-made-possible is the Crucifixion,[3] the very apex of the Great Story. Paul describes its *effect*: release from every form of oppression, whether based on spiritual condition, ethnicity, religion, gender, law, or social status; and beyond this, my redeeming as a true child and heir of God. This is God's ultimate redemptive agenda.

It begins to take place in me when I finally hear what he has been speaking to me over and over again—that I am *not* truly a slave, a reject, or even one who sincerely but unsuccessfully tries to do the right thing, but his child, the heir to all his goodness and glory. When I begin to live out this truth, I begin also to live redemption and justice into the world in which I dwell.

I get Paul's frustration when he writes, earlier in this same letter, "You foolish Galatians! Who has bewitched you? Before your very eyes Jesus Christ was clearly portrayed as crucified."[4] And later, "It is for freedom that Christ has set us free. Stand firm, then, and do not let yourselves be burdened again by a yoke of slavery."[5]

Paul had grown up a Jewish fundamentalist. He had been totally committed to Pharisaic dogma, could argue it vociferously, and was prepared to defend it with violence if necessary.

He was, before Jesus began to rip his arrogance from him, forging a successful career at doing so, a rising young star among his people. The process of redemption had been a painful one for him—the blinding recognition that a theology of power and control served himself and the status quo, not God; the loss of his own status, family connections, and probably a large chunk of his presumed identity; years spent in the relative wilderness of Arabia before even the Christians could get over their understandable skepticism about his conversion.

Along the way, he had come to realize that the systems and dogmas that had once defined him—the ones to which the Galatians were returning—had also trapped him. The freedom that Christ had purchased with his life had cost Paul most of what he had previously valued, but now he was glad to be rid of it, and determined never to submit himself to that kind of bondage again.[6]

I hear echoes of my own little story in the larger-than-life one of the apostle, and the still larger epic of the children of Israel.

There are many stories of redemption that are more dramatic than mine. Oppressive regimes have fallen because of the sacrificial acts of ordinary people who had discovered their true identity in Jesus; communities formerly crippled by poverty have been raised to new life because wealthy people from another nation sought to enact gospel justice. Afflicted inner-city neighborhoods have experienced healing because the people who live there began to view each other as brothers and sisters instead of as enemies.

Within my own community and circle of friends, there are extraordinary stories I could tell of men and women who, because of the abusive words and actions of their natural parents, became utterly lost in addictions, homelessness, prostitution, and even mental illness—people who, when they could go no further down, heard the voice of the loving Father, and were slowly transformed by the words he breathed.

But I'm selfish enough that I want to claim my own "normal," middle-class, First World story too. I also want and need this redeeming word, "You are my son!"[7] for my very own.

When, with the temerity of youth, I set myself against what I had come to regard as the exclusivist and unbiblical dogma of the church in which I had grown up, it did great damage to many of the relationships I valued most. I wrote a thesis about my views with the help of a cousin, and delivered it to the elders of my church. The paper became Exhibit A in the court of public opinion: although I, like Paul, had been a rising young star, I was now deemed a dangerous young man, possibly a heretic, almost overnight. I alienated my mother and father, my oldest brother, the older men and women I had so respected, and even my best friends.

That I even had the audacity to approach the issues I considered important is a testament to the securely confident home in which I grew up. I had been taught to think, to trust that the Bible really is God's Word, and that it was important to be right, particularly about theology, and to be willing to act on my convictions. When my older brother David left home at seventeen because of conflict with Dad, it only served (at the time) to confirm those convictions. I'm embarrassed to admit that, long before I decided that the rest of my family was wrong about most things, I had already managed to alienate Dave by my self-righteousness. (I'm happy to say we're good friends now.)

Imagine my shock, then, when my carefully researched and impeccably argued thesis (unassailable, I thought) was rejected out of hand, and my own reputation—not only at my own church but also within all those related to it across the country—went directly into the deepest, funkiest corner of the dumpster.

I didn't know it then, but God was beginning a process of redemption in my life. A process that has often felt more like radical surgery without anesthetic. I had thought it would be a constant strengthening, a wider scope of knowledge, a deeper certainty . . . instead, it has unfolded as the stripping away of all those things and more.

Here's the mystery of redemption: It may begin in a *moment* of deliverance, but its *effect* plays out over a lifetime of desert wandering. It turns suffering into glory, pain into peace, and dirt into gold—but it rarely looks like victory.

I left that church, believing I had no other choice. My father—a man of iron self-control—visited me one night, weeping and pleading with me to stay.

"Dad," I responded, "if anybody has taught me to obey what God teaches us in the Bible, it's you. That's what I'm trying to do."

I had already been cut off by my friends and mentors in that church, and so, wounded but still confident of my course, I walked.

I had been involved in various forms of outreach on the streets of the downtown core of Toronto from my teen years, and now I joined a band, Red Rain. We played in biker bars and jails, staying for many years far away from any venue run by Christians, convinced it was the best way to take the good news to the streets. Some years later, I began working full time as a "street pastor," and helped to plant and grow a community called Sanctuary—a community of people who desperately needed redemption.[8]

All through those years, my certainties about my own competence, fine points of doctrine, and how God operates were slowly being stripped away. I clung to them, believing them to be my salvation, and discovered when at last I reluctantly let go, a scrap at a time, I was being set free. My street-involved friends, wrecked by betrayals of what ought to have been their childhood innocence, were so profoundly lost in addictions, madness, and a bewildering, sordid array of other forms of oppression, that their neediness proved to me time and again the pathetic shallowness of my "answers."

Without even knowing the word, they cried out for *justice*—God's justice, which sees everything, releases the captive, and restores the slave; not the vengeful, punishing sort our society personifies as blindfolded and carrying a sword. In the process, they slowly uncovered my own deep need for that same redemption. We travel a seemingly limitless wilderness together, sustained by an unreasonable but growing hope that we are moving toward a promised land.

Through it all, my relationship with my father, and by extension, my mother and eldest brother, John, remained distant, strained. We took refuge in being polite, and kept our conversations short and shallow. It went on like that for more than twenty years.

When, some months before my father's death, a telephone conversation with my mother prompted me to finally admit that my marriage was failing, I seriously wondered if it would be the last brick in the wall between us. Knowing their deeply held convictions about the inviolability of marriage, and thinking they would believe the failure of mine to be the natural result of my willful wrongheadedness, I thought they just might finally wash their hands of me.

My mother stopped me in mid-sentence, and insisted on calling my father to join her on the phone. They listened attentively. My mother spoke compassionately, lovingly, and another piece of my armor was torn away. My father spoke little, if at all, that I remember—but I could hear him breathing heavily into the transceiver, and I knew his silence was not one of condemnation, but one of an aching heart.

In the ensuing months, my relationship with my parents became warmer than it had been in a great many years. Dad still didn't say much, but slowly we began to talk about the stuff that really mattered to us. The youngest of my mother's three boys, I had been quite close to her until the rift, and now our relationship began to blossom again.

That winter, John and I planned a summer cruise on Georgian Bay with my father, something we had never done before, although they had owned the boat together for quite a few years. But Dad died in the spring, and instead, John and I planned his funeral together. That might sound grim, but it was a surprisingly sweet experience.

We had never been close, my eldest brother and I. When I told him in the ICU waiting room that my wife and I had separated the day before Dad's accident, it was the first time I had ever spoken to him about our struggles. Standing at our father's bedside, and later, doing the rounds of funeral home, cemetery, church, and so on, a new bond was forged.

We talked openly about our respective relationships with our father, our own struggles and joys. We indulged ourselves in the kind of dark jokes that help people through terrible loss—it was tragic, we agreed, to be burying our seventy-nine-year-old father with a full head of black hair when both of us were balding. And when we did embark on that boat trip, just the two of us, we talked more and had more pleasure in each other's company during four days of puttering up rock-strewn channels, or anchored in the lee of an island while the sun scorched its setting path through wind-wild jack pines, than we had the whole of the forty-odd years of life we had previously shared.

In the days and months following Dad's death, my mother

and I found an unprecedented depth of intimacy too. Our aching hearts yearned toward each other as we puzzled out how we might live these new, peculiarly hollow lives, and at the same time wept and chuckled our way to a tender, mature enjoyment of each other that remains truly sweet. There was, at times, a nearly crippling loneliness, but even there, the seeds of redemption were already growing.

"In those early months," Mom told me later, "I think I was mostly numb. I didn't cry much. But when I'd been out somewhere, and came home, the place seemed so empty I'd burst into tears in the front hall. And I'd say to God, 'You promised you would never leave or forsake me. Well, I need you now like I never have before.' Then I'd go crawl into bed. And do you know, I could actually feel his arms around me. I've never before felt so close to him. It was the sweetest thing . . ."

Just a few days before the accident that took Dad's life, some of the family had gathered at his Muskoka cottage property to get it ready for summer use. Six Mile Lake was my father's favorite place on earth, and I don't think anything made him happier than working there. He took a genuine pleasure in seeing that others were working, too, and he was delighted with the progress we made in clearing the leaves, launching the boats, evicting the mice, and "putting the water in"—replanting the hoses and priming the pumps that draw water from the lake into the two cottages.

Dad found me alone at one point, and harrumphed the awkward question: What was happening with my marriage? When I told him that within a day or two we'd be telling the kids we were separating, he merely looked gravely at the ground and gave my arm a squeeze.

As we were leaving at day's end, my father thanked and congratulated each one for their good work, and gave them a hug. He wasn't really the hugging kind, my dad. It was his grandkids who taught him how, I think. His hugs were of the very manly kind—a hard, tight squeeze and a quick release.

I had noted with wonder his continued strength and vitality throughout the day. Seeing him stumble briefly while carrying a six-by-six beam, ten feet long, down a long flight of stairs, had only served to make me marvel that he could even lift the thing. I marveled again as I watched him hug Jesse, the only one of my children who had been able to come along. His grandson was a good four inches taller, and at least twenty pounds heavier, than he was himself, but Dad put his arms around Jesse and lifted him clear off the ground, spinning around in a circle as he did so.

Last of all, he came to me. He embraced me with a strange new tenderness, and, placing his cheek against mine, whispered into my ear.

"I'll be thinking of you."

It was the most intimate moment I had with my father in almost a quarter of a century. And they were the last words he ever spoke to me.

✠

Through the long desert of alienation and rejection, in the stripping away of dogmas and definitions I had thought would protect me, by deaths of shocking suddenness and bitter slowness, I am being made vulnerable enough to hear the rhythm of my Father's breath. He is redeeming me: the sin of my own arrogance and the oppression of dogma have less and less power to enslave. The healing of my family relationships in the midst of sorrow, failure, and loss is an echo of an even greater, eternal redemption.

This, then, is where my redemption story has brought me thus far. In both my earliest memory of my father, and in my last of him in living relationship, I am in his arms, and he is breathing blessing in my ear.

No longer slave, but son, inheritor of
all the Father's great goodness.

ELEVEN

TRAVELING TO CANAAN

My Beloved:

And when the Israelites saw the great power the LORD
displayed against the Egyptians, the people feared
the LORD and put their trust in him and in Moses his
servant.

Then Moses and the Israelites sang this song to
the LORD:

> "I will sing to the LORD,
>   for he is highly exalted.
> The horse and its rider
>   he has hurled into the sea.
> The LORD is my strength and my song;
>   he has become my salvation . . .

In your unfailing love you will lead
the people you have redeemed.
In your strength you will guide them
to your holy dwelling."

—FROM EXODUS, CHAPTERS 14 AND 15

How great is the love the Father has lavished on us,
that we should be called children of God! And that
is what we are! The reason the world does not know
us is that it did not know him. [*Beloved*], now we are
children of God, and what we will be has not yet been
made known. But we know that when he appears, we
shall be like him, for we shall see him as he is.

—FROM 1 JOHN, CHAPTER 3

Ray is old enough to be my father, I thought. *Why did they call me?*

Farms and woodlots rippled away from the highway as if a ribbon of asphalt had been poured onto the landscape just moments before my arrival. It was a perfect summer day: blue sky, high and wide, with the odd fleck of cloud drifting serenely about with no other function than to grant some scale to its limitlessness. The window of my little pickup was down, and each time I passed another dense copse of trees, I could at least imagine pine scent piercing the smell of hot tar and exhaust. There's almost always a speed trap on that stretch of road. I kept checking my speedometer to make sure I was staying right on that point where a cop would think about chasing me for a moment or two, but give it a pass in the confidence that a genuine road racer would be along shortly.

An hour later, my tires squonked to a tar-blistery stop outside the Midland Hospital. I fought my way into a blazer as I ran for the front doors.

It's never an encouraging sign when the ICU staff keeps close family members in the waiting room, but rushes the "pastor" directly to the patient's bedside. That blazer felt like a costume; I wasn't a pastor, really, but a young carpenter who sometimes preached at his home church, the church where Ray was a long-time, stalwart member. The nurse briefed me as she ushered me along.

Ray had a heart attack while puttering about on his beloved boat, at her berth in Midland Bay. It was serious; early indications were that there was a substantial amount of damage to the heart. They were having trouble getting Ray stabilized. He was terribly agitated, and kept insisting on seeing his pastor, even though the nurses told him he must stay calm. They were afraid he was on the verge of another attack, and pretty sure that if it came, it would be fatal. Please, would I do whatever I could to calm him down?

I felt even more like an impostor. *Impastor.*

Ray was that awful shade of gray: the color and slightly oily sheen of fresh putty, and that sheen was about the only thing that indicated he was still alive. Tubes everywhere, coming out his orifices and snaking ominously beneath the covers. Monitors blooping and bleeping away in their mysterious, unnerving code. His glasses and teeth had been removed. He looked ancient and shrunken and ready for the cooling board.

But when I called his name, his eyelids flew up like a pair of cheap blinds, and he began to get—*dang!*—agitated. I said inane young carpenter things in the most soothing voice I could find—*Hey, Ray, how's it goin', eh? Not so good, huh? Traffic was light coming north, though . . .*

By this time, Ray was starting to writhe around a bit, and nurses began to hover. It was clear, and understandable, I guess, that he wanted to cut to the chase.

It was like this: Ray was convinced he hadn't done enough. *Huh?*

Hadn't prayed enough, hadn't done enough Bible study, hadn't treated his wife and daughters as well as he should have (his eyes welling with sudden tears), hadn't believed hard enough, hadn't done enough work for the church . . .

I tried to slow him down by telling him that was absurd, but it didn't seem to help.

He hadn't done enough of anything that mattered, and now it looked like his time was up, and he was gonna die and go to hell, and how could he make it right with God?

The nurses weren't too impressed by my pastoral technique.

I was pretty rattled, too, I can tell you. I kept thinking, *Ray's going to die right in front of me, and I'll have to tell Helen and the girls that the last thing he said was, "I'm going to hell!"*

While Ray wasn't someone you'd ever mistake for a great spiritual leader, he was a good solid guy who had been married for thirty-odd years to the same woman, adored his daughters, and was well-liked by everybody. A decent, hardworking, blue-collar man—decades of service as a public school custodian—and a regular participant in most church functions. A guy who behaved and talked like a Christian at all times, as far as I could tell. Everybody I knew who knew Ray would have been gob-smacked by what he was saying.

I whipped out the ol' "Grace" package—God loves you so much that he gave his only Son to die for you—*you know this already, Ray*—and all you have to do is put your trust in him—*you've done that already, Ray! Haven't you?*—and he'll wash away all your sins. *Man, Ray, please don't tell me this is news!* You don't have to *do* anything. You *can't* do anything . . . I quoted the salient passages of Scripture, peering earnestly at my open Bible, blindly following my finger across the page so he'd know I wasn't just making it up.

The patient began to settle a bit, and so did the nurses. As soon as I could decently get clear of Ray, then his wife and daughters, I fled.

✠

The children of Israel must have been pretty rattled, too, when they saw the growing dust cloud behind them, then felt the vibration, heard the rumble of chariots, began to catch glimpses of spear heads flashing bright within the cloud. And realized, uh oh, the Red Sea is right in front of us . . .

The Exodus of more than a million people, all of them born into slavery, is one of the foundational redemption narratives of the Great Story. Although there are other hints of God's redemptive attempt earlier—Isaac being set free, and a ram taking his place as a sacrifice, for instance—the clear language of redemption begins here, when God instructs Moses to announce to the people, "I am the LORD, and I will bring you out from under the yoke of the Egyptians. I will free you from being slaves to them, and I will redeem you with . . . mighty acts of judgment."[1]

I will set you free. I will, by extravagant action, change the way you think of yourselves, and the way the Egyptians regard you. I will deem you anew. You will be no longer slaves, but my free people.

The story of the escape of a whole people from oppression, and their wandering search for a new home, has been replayed so many times throughout history (the Jews themselves lived it all over again through the first half of the twentieth century), and is such a great metaphor for the personal stories of billions of individuals, that it has become part of the fabric of western history and culture. Part of what makes it so great, and so accessible, is the wild raggedness of the story. It's not neat and easy, and even the Cecil B. DeMille epic left out a lot of the best bits.

There's the secret identity of the young prince, his

transformation into a rogue murderer, and subsequent exile in the back of beyond. His return, transformed yet again, as the reluctant savior of a weaponless, oppressed people. The struggle for freedom—nine false starts—is not primarily in military terms, but by means of bizarre and powerful magical acts that pit the one nameless God of the slaves against the rich pantheon of Egypt, the mightiest nation of the time. Finally, at the cost of the mysterious midnight slaughter of untold numbers of boys and young men, the people break loose—only to soon find they are trapped, threatened once more with slavery or death. One final miraculous, cataclysmic escape (a second slaughter of tens of thousands of Egyptians), and the people are free. Off they wander into the sunset, weary but hope filled, in search of the utopian home they know is out there somewhere. Whew.

Think about it. How many movies have you seen that use the same essential elements? Practically every sci-fi franchise ever produced, for starters.

But this, so far, is really only the introduction to the story of their redemption.

Standing on the far bank of the Red Sea, with wooden shields and the shafts of broken spears still bobbing about on its now placid surface, Moses and his sister Miriam, together with the entire mob of ex-slaves, break into song. (Okay, that doesn't happen very often in sci-fi movies.) They sing the story of the great deliverance they have just experienced, and praise their Deliverer. It's not until halfway through their lengthy ballad that they identify why God even bothered:

In your unfailing love you will lead
the people you have redeemed . . .

And in the very next phrase, they foretell the rest of the story. I mean the rest of the whole human story, the Great Story, together with my little story, not just the tale of the Israelites:

In your strength you will lead them to your holy dwelling.

Gods, in that era, were generally viewed as dangerously powerful, largely amoral, and often a little on the grumpy side as regards mere mortals. It was generally best to escape their notice entirely, if possible, and to placate them, if not. The Israelites must have done a lot of wondering about why a God powerful enough to defeat the Egyptians all on his own would decide to take up the cause of a people who had already been slaves for four hundred years. There was no discernible benefit in it for him. They puzzled and pondered, and finally concluded that there was only one motivation that made sense.

He loved them!

How strangely wonderful was that? And because they figured this Yahweh must love them, they knew that he wouldn't just set them free, pat them on their bums, and say, "Run along now. I've given you a fresh start—see what you can make of it. I know it's a desert, but you'll find something."

Nope. He would lead them home. And not just to their own home, but to his!

By "purchasing" a nation of slaves and setting them free, God certainly enacted redemption in its most classic form. A *moment* of redemption. But the *effect* of it was a long way from being complete as the people sang and danced their praise and (I imagine) made rude gestures toward the shocked remnant of the Egyptian army on the far bank.

The part of the story in which I hear echoes of my own tale, and Ray's, is in the journey from that point until they finally enter the promised land. The people grumble. They complain about the food and water. They want to go back to Egypt, take refuge in a slavery that is at least familiar. They get all dramatic, and wail that they're going to die there in the desert. When Moses goes up the hill to get the commandments, they get bored and make up their own god.

I do all of this same stuff.

And when finally, miraculously, they arrive at the border of Canaan after escaping the oppression of the world's most powerful regime, eating and drinking well all the way across the desert, defeating enemies, and in possession of the world's most comprehensive, egalitarian religious, civil, and criminal code—they're too afraid to walk in and claim what God has promised. They had hooted and hollered about how strong he was, and how in that strength he'd lead them home . . . *but the people down there in Canaan, they're kinda large, see* . . .

They couldn't escape their slave mentality, even though they had escaped their slave masters. They turned tail, and scampered back out into the desert. So deeply ingrained was the sense that good things were not for them that they wandered in circles for another thirty-eight years. All but two of the people who had experienced that initial redemption died in the wilderness; it was a new generation—a generation not born in slavery—that finally claimed the land.

It took all that time for them to hear the voice of God redeeming them:

You are not slaves! You are free; you are my children,
and I love you . . .

Although Ray had spent most of a lifetime following God through the desert toward his "holy dwelling," he panicked, and was afraid to claim it as he stood on the threshold because he had not been listening to that gentle Voice. Ray forgot who he really was.

The apostle John was also afraid that his disciples—faced with their own failures and insufficiencies, and distracted by both the attractions and challenges of the world around them—would forget who they really were. *See that what you have heard from the beginning remains in you. If it does, you also will remain in the Son and in the Father,*[2] he told them.

John had grown up with the story of the Exodus, and had witnessed the great moment that is the crux of all redemption, both past and future. He had heard the voice of the One who hung on the cross redeeming him: *You are now the son of my mother!* Now he urged his followers to remember what the Spirit had breathed into them at the beginning of their own redemption story, and to keep listening.

He had learned, through his long life, filled with loss and persecution, the great beauty and power of love. I might expect him to say, "God loves us because we are his children," but John knew that, in the economy of the One Who Is Love, the order is different. *Because he loves us, he has called us his children.*

He warns me not to be surprised if this doesn't make sense to other people; if they are not themselves listening for the sound of God breathing, they will not hear this redeeming word. *Beloved* is how John addresses the people to whom he writes, and so reminds them, and me, that we are beloved of God.[3] The transformation that this love effects is still not done: *what we will be is not yet known . . .*

✠

Years later, I visited Ray again in a hospital room. In the interim, I actually had become a kind of pastor to him and his family. The words I had spoken to him in the ICU in Midland—the echo of a Voice he had known long since—seemed to have taken root after all. I had presided over the funeral of his father, and spent time with him and his wife in the wake of an auto accident that had left Helen legally blind and with some impairment of her cognition and short-term memory. His tenderness and complete devotion to her up until his final illness had been touching to witness.

This time there was no question but that Ray was dying. Abdominal pain had at first made him think maybe his heart was acting up again, but tests provided a different and discouragingly conclusive answer: Ray had liver cancer. He had only weeks to live.

On the day of my visit, Ray had been in the hospital a little more than two weeks, and he'd be gone in less than one more. He was in excruciating pain, a pain that morphine could barely blunt. The whole time I was with him, his body was in almost constant, writhing motion, seeking fruitlessly for a position that would offer some relief.

Yes, he was agitated. But now it was exclusively a physical condition. Never have I seen a greater dichotomy between a tortured body and a soul at peace.

He smiled as best he could when I entered the room, and listened to my pleasantries for a minute or two, and then, just as he had so many years before, he cut to the chase.

There were some things he wanted me to know. He knew he was dying, that he had very little time left. Yes, he was concerned about his girls, and his grandkids, and especially his beloved Helen, of course. *But something wonderful was happening.*

God had been speaking to him, visiting him. Telling him over and over, in the midst of his agony, *I love you*. Telling him everything would be okay, that he was taking Ray home. *I love you.* You have nothing to fear. You're my child. *I love you*, and nothing will ever change that . . .

"Greg," Ray gasped, "it's so sweet. These past two weeks." Waving his hand weakly to indicate his heaving body, and the medical trappings of the last earthly room he would ever see. "It's all worth it . . ."

✠

Each time I find myself in a new phase of life, I become aware that the period I have just passed out of—the period in which I thought, "This is it! This is what I'm here for!"—was really mostly a preparation for where I am now. By this, I become aware that redemption is at work in me, turning the junk of the past into treasure. This is the power of redemption. It doesn't merely release me from slavery, but sets me on the path to a true home. It not only heals, but gives a previously unknown strength too. The very locus of suffering becomes a place of glory.

I wonder, sometimes, should I be aware at the last that I haven't long to live, if I will be delivered into a moment of awesome clarity, the understanding that the whole journey up until now has been for the purpose of bringing me to *this* moment. In that moment, I will hear it; no longer a quiet breath, but a joyful summons, deeming me—

My Beloved.

TWELVE

Plastic Pop Bottles

My Pleasure:

Now the tax collectors and "sinners" were all
gathering around to hear him. But the Pharisees and
the teachers of the law muttered, "This man welcomes
sinners and eats with them."

Then Jesus told them this parable: "Suppose one
of you has a hundred sheep and loses one of them.
Does he not leave the ninety-nine in the open country
and go after the lost sheep until he finds it? And when
he finds it, he joyfully puts it on his shoulders and goes
home. Then he calls his friends and neighbors together
and says, 'Rejoice with me; I have found my lost sheep.'

"Or suppose a woman has ten silver coins and
loses one . . ."

—FROM THE GOSPEL OF LUKE, CHAPTER 15

A young boy, standing on the corner of a busy downtown street on a summer evening in 1988. He's wearing cut-off jean shorts, the tip of one pocket showing beneath the white fringe of frayed fabric, a tight T-shirt and a ball cap perched jauntily on the back of his head. He can't be more than twelve or thirteen, he's small for his age, and cute as a button.

There is a steady thrum of traffic northbound on Bay Street. All the unlucky, slightly less than necessary drones from the bank towers have finally been set free for the weekend. Their bosses departed midday for their fabulous vacation properties in that part of the Muskokas where "cottage" means a million-dollar fantasy home. The drones are eager to be gone from the city, too, if they have a place to go—or to get home, showered, and changed so they can get back downtown to the clubs or to a buddy's backyard for barbecue and beer.

The boy is standing ten or fifteen feet back from the corner. There is a hospital on this street, and a parking garage and some government buildings, so lots of cars turn off of Bay onto Grosvenor. Every once in a while, one of those cars veers to the curb and slows to a crawl as it passes the boy. He steps forward, bobbing toward each car, peeking into its window. Stepping back and straightening up as they pull away.

The boy is humming. Absentmindedly, little scraps of a melody. Every now and then he opens his mouth and begins to sing, softly, to himself. With the traffic noise you'd have to be standing right beside him to hear the words.

Amazing grace, how sweet the sound . . .

It seems odd that a young boy would be singing the classic hymn of the tired, world-weary sinner, but it is a beautiful melody.

A nameless sedan swings to the curb beside the boy and stops. He bobs; the passenger window hums down into the door. The boy ceases singing, and reaches for the handle.

The man behind the wheel is well dressed in conventional business attire. Old enough that he's probably made some kind of peace with being stuck in the middle floors of the gleaming towers to the south. A cubicle dweller.

He smiles, places a large hand on the boy's bare thigh.

"How much?" he asks.

The houses in my old neighborhood all have front porches. Some years ago, walking past a house a couple of streets away, I noticed, hanging above the railing of its porch, a couple of bird feeders. They had been crafted from large plastic pop bottles. *Simple and clever,* I thought. A week or so later, I happened to be walking by again. The porch was now filled with bird feeders, all made from plastic pop bottles, in an astonishing range of designs and decorations.

They were delightful. I wondered why whoever had made them had taken time to craft so many, each one apparently unique. Most people just toss those bottles in the recycling bin without a further thought. Even if the feeders were for sale, there couldn't have been enough money in them to make the effort economically worthwhile.

It seems to me that a person who takes the time to create a beautiful, original bird feeder out of something as apparently valueless as a disposable plastic bottle is one who delights not only in feeding birds, but in reclaiming and reinventing stuff. In fact, my guess is that it's not about the birds at all. It's about the sheer pleasure to be found in redeeming something other people can only see as junk.

That's God all over.

From the early movements of the Great Story, he's had a thing for the underdog. Jacob—the younger, weaker son who will become the father of the children of Israel—is a shiftless momma's boy who is eager and willing to shaft his older brother. His very name means "the crook." But God blesses him with wealth and a large family anyway. Turns out, though, that Jacob has spawned a brood of vicious, petty lunkheads who sell their younger brother, Joseph, into slavery out of mere spite.

God rescues the young slave and ultimately turns him into the prime minister of the world's first superpower. Jacob, now sometimes called Israel ("the one who struggles with God"), has by this time become a weak-witted geezer presiding over a family so dysfunctional (incest, prostitution, murder, and more) that they'd be a hit on prime-time television. A famine forces him and his brood to move to Egypt, where he'll receive food and protection from his long-lost son—but doom his family to four hundred years of slavery as a result.

Really. This is the best God can do for his "chosen people"?

Even once the people settle in the promised land, they never really become anything to write home about. Scrapping and squabbling among themselves, paying tribute to other larger, better organized nations. They do hit a brief peak during the reigns of David (a murderer and adulterer) and Solomon (a smart guy, for sure, but one who, like many political leaders, apparently couldn't control himself sexually), but immediately afterward the nation descends into civil war, splits in two, and spends the next eight hundred years under the thumb of a succession of oppressors before being dismantled entirely.

God sends a Messiah, a savior of the people. The Jews (the tribes of Judah and Benjamin; the ten other tribes have by this point gone completely missing) have been waiting for this hero to appear, and the timing couldn't be better. Each successive oppressor has gotten larger, stronger; Rome is the King Kong of empires. The Messiah will set the people free, like Moses, and reestablish Israel among the nations, reigning with the glory of Solomon on the throne of David.

Or maybe not. He dies as a common criminal, a flea on the backside of Rome. His followers, a gaggle of uncouth backcountry rabble-rousers, will be executed or dispersed, and the iconic city Jerusalem razed to the ground.

Talk about backing a loser.

And that's just the biblical story. The chosen people will spend the next nineteen hundred years in persecuted homelessness. Every time they land somewhere they think they might put down roots, somebody new makes it a personal mission to destroy them. Even the institutions of the "new" religion founded by their own people hunt them down. When, finally, a handful do find their way back to the historic homeland, the world around them has expanded dramatically. Their country is now a tiny little slice of desert perched precariously on the sea into which their many cranky neighbors would love to push them. They don't even have any oil . . .

The only indications that they just might be "chosen" by God, apart from the Bible saying that he says so, are that a) they've actually survived; and b) they are, as a people, the most potent source of theology, philosophy, art, literature, and science that the world has ever known.

When Jesus tells the story of the lost sheep, he's speaking to a group of successful leaders who lead the good life. Despite their own national history, they can't figure out why this young teacher, who so obviously has great potential, prefers to hang out with such losers. His answer is surprisingly simple: it makes him happy.

Nobody takes any real notice of a plastic pop bottle when it's full—it's the contents we want, and when we're done, we discard the container. Jesus says he loves taking that old bottle, and turning it into something fun and enduringly useful, something that will bless the birds for a long time to come. He takes pleasure in doing it. Recovering the lost sheep gives him a reason to have a party with his friends. It's far more enjoyable than sitting there watching the other ninety-nine chew their cud.

He's so determined to make his point that he tells two more versions of the story—a woman who has lost some money and throws a party when she finds it again; and most famously, a man whose reprobate son returns, prompting a massive celebratory feast.

It would be good business to write off the one lost sheep, rather than risk the rest of the flock. It doesn't make sense to spend the money you just found on throwing a party—you're still out the money, aren't you? All well and good to welcome the prodigal home, but why not take him in quietly, make sure he's for real this time, and avoid reinforcing his delinquent behavior by throwing a big bash?

I can almost hear God say, "I know. But it makes me happy!"

It's so easy, whether I'm wallowing in my failures or congratulating myself on my successes, to miss this gentle, delightful message. There's a lightness to it that balances my tendency to take myself or the world around me too seriously.

Paul says this has been God's approach all along: "He chose us in him before the creation of the world to be holy and blameless in his sight. In love he predestined us to be adopted as his sons through Jesus Christ, in accordance with his pleasure and will . . . And he made known to us the mystery of his will according to his good pleasure . . ."[1]

The young boy, Leonard, who stood on the street corner singing hymns, is a close friend of mine. A family life so confused and sordid that it would have fit perfectly in the Old Testament prepared him for and pushed him toward street prostitution when he was still really just a child. That's where he stayed for the best part of ten years, and although I've heard the stories, I can't begin to imagine the scope of destruction he endured, or how he managed to survive.

It would be many more years before my friend became a Christian. That he did, I think, is a miracle of the highest order. Through his years on the street, he had sung hymns and cried out to God to rescue him, but God, as far as he or anyone else could tell, never responded. If it had been me, the bitterness of the image of a child singing "'Tis grace has brought me safe thus far" as he climbs into the car of yet another man who will abuse him might well have burned right out of me any shred of belief in a loving, just, and merciful God.

Instead, when Leonard now looks back on his singing "Amazing Grace" to comfort himself as he stood waiting for another car to pull over, he regards it as a prophetic word to his future adult self that God never did abandon him. One small evidence of the power of redemption to reach backward, into the history of our lives.

"I used to sing 'Softly and Tenderly,'" my friend tells me. "But mostly I would sing 'Amazing Grace.' They made me think of my grandmother, who loved me no matter what. I sang them because I felt that though I was a sinner, maybe God could still care about me, like my grandma did."

Leonard is an amazing guy. His story is a testimony to the tenacity and reach of God's redemptive agenda in an individual life, and to his own extraordinary faith. And yet, despite the years that have passed and the phenomenal progress he's made, elements of his story still represent a terrible danger to him.

Through the years Leonard has told his story to many people. Local high school students and people visiting Sanctuary from all over North America have been captivated by the drama of his tale. (I have sketched it here in merest strokes.) They are amazed by his faith and courage, and perhaps drawn by the vicarious thrill of anecdotes in which tragedy of the most ignoble kind gives way to a quiet triumph, embodied by the small, warmly affectionate man telling the story.

Not long ago, Leonard's street past came rearing up out of the depths and bit him with a surprising swiftness and ferocity. It's naïve, I suppose, for any of us to think that our past is ever, in this life, truly, finally past.

As his friends and faith family have walked alongside Leonard in this latest challenge, it has become clear to some of us that the constant retelling of his story, which we had thought was an evidence of the depth of his healing, was in fact doing him great damage. Constantly recounting the painful scenarios of his early years seemed to reinforce that old identity: prostitute, boy-toy, worthless street kid. Some of those old behaviors began to creep up on him again. The volume of his own voice, recounting to fascinated audiences how he had been stripped of his essential human dignity and used as an object of pleasure, slowly drowned out the quieter, deeper Voice that whispered,

I came to find you when you were lost. To me, you are holy and blameless. Because I love you, I decided long ago to adopt you, knowing that your own family would betray and abuse you. Doing this delights me—you delight me! There is no greater pleasure to me than redeeming—remaking, renaming—the one who has been lost or cast aside. Listen to me: you know this already. It is a mystery no longer. You're my son, my beloved, and I am carrying you home, rejoicing all the way.

Leonard had been deeming himself, long after it had ceased to be fact, a child prostitute, a mere instrument of pleasure to be used and discarded by conscienceless men. Although my childhood was, by comparison to his, one of privilege and tender care, there have been so many failures, faults, and dysfunctions in my life (that wide range of weakness and wrongheadedness that is summed up by the biblical writers with the simple word *sin*) that I, too, am in danger of deeming myself as defined by them. In doing so, I relinquish to them a power over my actions and identity that they should not have.

Our Sanctuary community includes people like me, with privileged backgrounds and current circumstance; people like Leonard, who have experienced extraordinary salvation from horrific situations; and many who are still wandering in the wilderness of addictions, prostitution, and a great many other ills. All of us struggle with this. We talk often about not listening to the voices—within and without—that condemn us, but listening instead to the redeeming Voice.

It's easy to get lost in all those impossible "why" questions—why did this happen to me? Why should an innocent child like Leonard be subjected to such horror? Why the latest natural disaster, and all the human tragedies that flow from it?

But asking "Why?" is a fruitless endeavor.

Redemption is not God's answer to why; it is his response to the horrors that prompt the question. Redemption is why God's people need to seek justice for people who are abused, excluded, oppressed, depressed, afflicted, and destitute. This is how followers of Jesus are supposed to live out the good news.[2]

It's so easy to get lost in the details of my own story, the little hooks and hitches, the many obligations and small fictions out of which I fabricate the identity I wear for myself and others. This "coat" I put on so long ago has become heavy, stifling. It constricts my movements and disguises my true shape, but its familiarity is so powerful that I can hardly imagine taking it off. The freedom might feel like vulnerability, and I'm not sure who I might turn out to be. That gentle breath slowly strips away the fictions of my worthlessness, my disposability. It fashions for me a new and truer identity, clothes me in fresh garments, light as a whisper.

You are my child, my love—come, rejoice with me!

Part Five

CONSUMMATION

THIRTEEN

ABOARD THE *AMADEUS*

My Child:

But now, this is what the LORD says—
    he who created you, O Jacob,
    he who formed you, O Israel:
    "Fear not, for I have redeemed you;
    I have summoned you by name; you are
    mine . . .
Since you are precious and honored in my
    sight, and because I love you,
I will give men in exchange for you,
    and people in exchange for your life.
Do not be afraid, for I am with you;
    I will bring your children from the east
    and gather you from the west.

I will say to the north, 'Give them up!'
    and to the south, 'Do not hold them
    back.'
Bring my sons from afar
    and my daughters from the ends of the
    earth—everyone who is called by my
    name,whom I created for my glory,
    whom I formed and made."

—FROM ISAIAH, CHAPTER 43

He who was seated on the throne said, "I am making
everything new!" Then he said, "Write this down,
for these words are trustworthy and true." He said to
me, "It is done. I am the Alpha and the Omega, the
Beginning and the End. To him who is thirsty I will
give to drink without cost from the spring of the water
of life. He who overcomes will inherit all this, and I
will be his God and he will be my son."

—FROM REVELATION, CHAPTER 21

I am standing at the helm of an early-nineteenth-century
ship: a brig, or perhaps a small frigate. Although she is
so old, everything about her is in perfect condition:

her brightwork gleams, the shrouds, sheets, and halyards are flawlessly exact, her sails are like dunes of snow against a sapphire sky. On her stern is the name, in letters of flowing gold, *Amadeus*. Every hum of the rigging, every snap of luffing canvas, each creak of every timber sings a symphony of joy as if the spirit of Mozart himself were the breeze that propels us.

The ship curtseys gently into each long trough, then raises her bowsprit again with pride as she meets the swell. Her happiness runs like a current along her waterline, bubbling busily around the rudder, vibrating upward and into the palms of my hands upon the spokes of her wheel.

There is a wide hammock swinging gently just an arm's length from the helm and in it, stretching with a delicious languor, is my sweet and beautiful wife, Maggie. She is wearing the pretty little sundress she wore on our honeymoon, and a small smile, and she is being careful not to spill a drop of the delicious and particularly intoxicating fruity concoction that she balances in a goblet upon her belly.

The waist deck below is a tilting field of teak plank, faded to an opalescent dove grey. On it stands a harvest table laden with hillocks of food on elegant dishes, and silver and crystal ware that cast wild beams of reflected and refracted sunlight against the screen of the mainsail. By some magic, nothing else on the table moves, not even the wine in tall crystal decanters, or the soup that steams in a tureen large enough to bathe a baby in.

My father is at the table, slowly sharpening a knife— I can hear the *shshoop* of the blade against the steel—and contemplating how best to begin carving the roast beast before him. My mother appears, delivering an elaborate dessert. She puts it down with a tiny frown. I know she is wondering if the meringue will really stay nice and crisp in this heat and humidity. Both of them are as I remember them when I was a child: vigorous, graceful, possessed of a lightness that probably only truly exists in memory or dreams.

Suddenly I realize that the ship is full of souls, all the ones I have ever loved or wanted to love. My brothers John and David, and their families. Lifelong friends like Kevin, childhood pals like Mark, whom I haven't seen in most of a lifetime, my brothers and sisters from the Sanctuary community.

The band is on the poop deck behind me; by a miracle only a musician could appreciate, there is no PA, there are no electrical cords—but everything can be heard with perfect clarity. Dan's Telly is pouring notes into a sky as blue as the music, Doug and Les are laying down a groove the ship seems to be sailing on, and Phil's big fat B3 sound is like a tide of aural honey. I am singing a song I have never known before, and I can hit notes as deep as a whale, or as high, sweet, and pure as a meadowlark. In the waist, Annie and Sharon, and now Maggie, too, are dancing.

Marty and April and Smurf and Lenny and California and Billy and Tony and Gracie and Marcel and dozens, dozens of other friends from the street, gone too long and too soon, are skylarking in the rigging, dancing high above the decks . . . There must be thousands of people on board, but there is space to spare on this small ship.

And my children are here. Oh, my children are here. Tanned

and laughing, glowing as if from within, giggling and falling all over each other as they so often do. I realize that, although I am still at the helm, since this is my dream, they are handling the sails. Furling an unnecessary canvas here, loosening a sheet there. We are sailing this ship together.

Maggie's children are here too: Cam, Reid, and Gillian. Younger than my adult children, they watch tentatively at first but soon they, too, are anticipating each needed shift of the canvas, and flitting about the rigging as if they were born to be jack tars.

Our children.

On the *Amadeus*, every division of my life has been reconciled, every broken relationship healed. All the neediness of my own soul, and the souls of the people I love, has been met and overwhelmed by the Great Love.

Just over the horizon, I know, is an island of tall palm trees, with a white beach and a coral lagoon. We will drop anchor in its turquoise water, and eat and drink as the sun slips toward the sea, gilding a path from the far horizon to the glittering water lapping against our hull. As a velvet night falls, we'll light many lanterns, then slide down the anchor chain to swim in a silken sea.

It might be hard to believe, given the silly extravagance of the "dream" above, but I'm not a particularly fanciful person. I don't usually go off on wild flights of imagination, or even spend much time anticipating holidays or other special events, although I certainly value and enjoy them when they arrive. I suppose I'm generally too preoccupied with daily events to daydream.

But the denouement of the Great Story is the stuff of heroic dreams: a city of gems and golden streets descending from heaven; choirs made up of millions of people, angels, and magical beasts; the King of kings, Great Warrior of Heaven, riding a white horse triumphantly through the clouds. That same King, the Author of the Great Story, crowned with glory, pulling me out of the watching crowd, placing his hand on my shoulder and announcing to his Father, loud enough for all to hear, "This is the child you gave to me."

And to me: "Little brother, this is my Father, and your Father, the Great I Am."[1]

It's like something out of the final scenes of *The Lord of the Rings*, only more so. The only way I can access it is by imagination. I think part of the point of these extravagant tableaux is that I should be prompted to wonder—both the kind of wonder that prompts me to say, "Could it be like this, or will it be like that?" and the kind that causes me to ooh and aah! My "dream" is the result of taking a few hours to wonder what perfect, complete consummation might appear like to me as a child myself, as a parent of children, and as a husband, a lover.

This *consummation*, in the larger theological sense, is the drawing together of all the necessary disparate elements to arrive at a perfect fulfillment of God's design for all creation.

The biblical sketches of this end-which-is-a-beginning are, I'm convinced, just that—merest line drawings, scribbles on a sketch pad of an infinite landscape. My own version is so small, so egocentric, that it's actually a little embarrassing to relate.

As Isaiah prophesied to the nation of Israel in ancient times, I feel the breath of God in my ears, addressing both my earthbound self—O Jacob! O Crooked One, Miserable Wanderer!—and the part of me that wrestles with imagining something greater—O Israel! O Struggler with God, Seeker of Blessing! The big story of a whole nation, its fear of being left alone, a defenseless child, to walk through trials, and of losing its sons and daughters, is my small, personal story too. It's interesting that in this prophecy, as in most others, God speaks as if talking directly to an individual although he is addressing an entire nation.

The very first words of this consummation promise are directed at the most insecure part of me. Before the Lord even opens his mouth, the prophet reminds me that the One about to speak is the One who created me in all my Jacob-ness— my foolishness, my blindness, my grasping selfishness. He has formed me also in my Israel-ness—my desire to do and be better, live bigger, and to reach for God himself. He knows me in every extreme, and still calls me "precious and honored," and proclaims his love for me.

Don't be afraid. Remember? God says. *I have redeemed you, and I'm calling you by that new name, calling you close. No matter how hard you may try to sell yourself to someone else, and sabotage all that awaits you, you belong to me.*

He promises, because of this, to continue that redeeming work, ransoming me in the most extravagant terms.

And now the consummation promise: he will gather his children—me! my children!—from the ends of the earth, wherever they have wandered or been driven, setting them free from whatever bonds may constrain them, and he will bring them home. He will call them by his own name—take them into his family—and it will become plain that they were created to live in his glory, made to look like him.

I have never encountered a family within which there is not some measure of pain and alienation. I have known far too many where the destruction is active and intense. Many people in my community have been so badly abused as children by parents that it has made a wreck of their entire lives. One such friend, who has battled long and hard against addiction, winning enormous victories at great cost, was faced recently with the impending death of his father. One part of him wanted to dance on the evil old man's grave; another wept for fear of losing his dad. What he truly longed for most was some kind of acknowledgment from his father of the great damage that had been done, so that he could extend forgiveness, and they could be reconciled at the last.

The promise of consummation begins where we begin to live—in family. I hear the promise to bring the children home both as a parent who aches for his children, and as a child who desires perfect harmony with his parents.

My "dream" of consummation reveals some interesting things to me about my deep longings.

I love sailing, and the romance of old ships. I never feel so free as when, under sun and sail, I can see blue water meet blue sky in an everlasting kiss. It whispers eternity to me, and eternal love. *Amadeus*, Latin for "Beloved of God," is a name I might have chosen for myself. I love both the tragic story and the glorious music of Mozart.

Maggie's presence is natural, immediate, necessary. In my imagination, she is there from the beginning. She has worked so hard through many long difficult years that it's a delight to see her at rest, and sheer joy to have her beside me.

It's fascinating to me to notice that, other than Maggie, the first people to "appear" in my dream are my parents. While there has been much healing in our relationships, I long for the perfect harmony that can only be found in this ultimate consummation of all things. I long for this deeper movement also in my relationship with my brothers, with whom I have only really had intimate friendship in recent years. In that place, my parents, my brothers, and I will all be sons and daughters, ransomed out of slavery and brought from afar by our Brother, to rest beneath the smiling benedictions of a greater Father and Mother.

My mates in the band, my brothers and sisters on staff and in the broader community of Sanctuary, and other old friends, have long been so central in my life that I can't imagine this voyage without them. Curiously, although I am an introvert who loves solitude, my dream is of a large community, traveling together like a kind of mobile village, toward a perfect destination where our hunger will be sated.

As dear as these friends are, there are many unresolved matters between us. It's the nature of humanity; in fact, there are times when insisting on resolving issues only makes things worse. And beyond these good friends, maybe way up in the rigging or in cabins down below, are those many relationships that have been lost through conflict, time, or distance, and which I still grieve. In many of these cases, there may be little or no real reconciliation in the world I inhabit now—the best we may do is an absence of conflict—but the future consummation that God promises calls me to live in hope that both the small fractures and the dramatic breaks will someday be healed.

The presence of many friends who have died street-related deaths—murder, suicide, overdose, AIDS, the cumulative effect of years of self-abuse—is a reminder that their tragic stories haunt me still, and that I yearn for some final, godly justice for lives that sometimes seemed cursed from the beginning.

But the very apex of my longing for this consummation is represented by the appearance, at last, of Maggie's children and mine.

It's right and good, I suppose, that parents are more deeply and continually concerned about their children than they are about anyone else. That's a generalization, of course; my community is full of people whose mental, spiritual, and material poverty is the disastrous result of their parents' lack of concern.

It's a curious thing. We spend our energy on trying to cultivate enough strength of character and breadth of learning that our children can become independent, but fear losing them. When they're little, we're afraid they'll be hurt or snatched;

when they're adults, we're afraid they'll forget about us, or see us as out of touch and irrelevant. But mostly we just hunger for the best possible things for our children, whatever their ages.

Our deep desire, Maggie's and mine, for consummation in the lives of our children is given an extra *frisson* of anxiety and longing because both of us have come from broken marriages. As bitter as the experience has been for us, we have come through it, found healing (imperfect though it may be) and great delight in each other.

For our children, it's another story. As ever, they are the ones who pay the stiffest price for the faults of their parents. Perhaps it's not so much a curse, but an observation, that the sins of the fathers will be visited upon their children.[2]

We feel so keenly that our failures as spouses and parents have left our kids living a brokenness that can never be fully repaired. Try as we might, we cannot fix it for them. I do trust that God can redeem it for them, and his redemption is such a miraculous thing that great strength may be forged out of weakness, and something even better than the original may grow.

We yearn not for a patching up, a repair of the broken bits that will allow our children to stagger through life, but for the gathering together of all the disparate elements of their personal and our collective experience, from the brightest to the darkest, into a new and consummate reality for all of us. When I meet Caleb, Kelly, and Rachel for brunch at the restaurant where she works, or call Jesse in Ottawa, four hours' drive away, and I see and hear how beautiful they are, and how gracious they are to me, I ache for this. I know Maggie feels the same way when the time rolls around for Cam, Reid, and Gilly to make the weekly switch, returning to the home of their father.

It's with deep gratitude, then, that I hear the Spirit whisper the promise of consummation. I want to live my life now toward this future reality. At the end of all things, as John the Revelator describes it, the One who is seated on the throne will not promise to repair the damage, but will declare, *I am making all things new!* It is he, I realize at last, who is really captain of the *Amadeus*. It's he who will pilot us into that perfect lagoon, and declare that it is time for the feast to begin.

You need not fear the end, he tells me, *for I* am *both Beginning and End.*

Then every person on board—my parents, my brothers, friends, Maggie and I, and our children—will hear him say,

I am your God, and you are my son.

FOURTEEN

Erotica

My Love:

Let him kiss me with the kisses of his mouth—
    for your love is more delightful than wine.
Pleasing is the fragrance of your perfumes;
    your name is like perfume poured out.
    No wonder the maidens love you!
Take me away with you—let us hurry!
    Let the king bring me into his chambers.

—from Solomon's Song of Songs, chapter 1

Then I heard what sounded like a great multitude,
like the roar of rushing waters and like loud peals of
thunder, shouting:

"Hallelujah!
For our Lord God Almighty reigns.
Let us rejoice and be glad
    and give him glory!
For the wedding of the Lamb has come,
    and his bride has made herself ready."

Then I saw a new heaven and a new earth, for the first
heaven and the first earth had passed away, and there
was no longer any sea. I saw the Holy City, the new
Jerusalem, coming down out of heaven from God,
prepared as a bride beautifully dressed for her husband.
And I heard a loud voice from the throne saying, "Now
the dwelling of God is with men, and he will live with
them. They will be his people, and God himself will be
with them and be their God."

One of the seven angels who had the seven bowls full
of the seven last plagues came and said to me, "Come,
I will show you the bride, the wife of the Lamb." And
he carried me away in the Spirit to a mountain great
and high, and showed me the Holy City, Jerusalem,
coming down out of heaven from God. It shone with
the glory of God, and its brilliance was like that of a
very precious jewel . . .

—FROM REVELATION, CHAPTERS 19 AND 21

S eriously, now. What's the first thing you think of when you hear or read the word *consummation*?

Uh huh.

Recently, I officiated at the wedding of a truly lovely young couple. They're passionate about each other, and passionate about God. Both have already shown that they're deeply committed followers of Jesus; they're involved in urban mission work now, and talking about becoming missionaries in the Muslim world in a few years.

Every week or so, during the months before the wedding, I would greet the bride, "So, Em, are you excited?" Her face would light up, and she would respond, "I'm *sooooo* excited!"

It was true. Em and her groom were so eager to tie the knot that I found both of them swanning around the sanctuary of the church an hour before the wedding was to take place, greeting the gaggle of very early arrivals, just generally looking beautiful and as if they were ready to explode. The wedding ran its flawless course (but for the soggy carpet in the south aisle, where the heating pipes had burst overnight), followed by the taking of many pictures, the eating of a great deal of exemplary baking, and some standing around. Then the wedding party, their parents, and a handful of friends repaired to a restaurant not far away for supper.

As the delightful evening wound on, I found myself watching the young couple, and thinking of consummation. I was pretty sure that, as excited as they had been about the wedding, it was the marriage itself they were really after, and that by this time they'd be about ready to leave the party and get down to the business of consummating it.

☩

The "Beloved" who sings a duet with her "Lover" in the astonishingly erotic song-poem, *Solomon's Song of Songs*, is one eager girl herself. Characterized as a young, poor shepherdess in love with a wealthy, powerful, and equally besotted king, she starts right off by begging her lover to kiss her in that crazily intoxicating way he does.

He smells great!

Even his name is sweet! (Can you imagine her, when she's alone, whispering it to herself over and over, like a prayer?)

She even boosts his ego a bit, as if the king needs ego boosting. She can hardly contain herself. She's out of her mind with desire . . . *Please, baby, can't we go* now? *Oh, take me to your room!*

You can practically hear her growling.

And that's just the first half of the opening chapter. Her lover, when he finally responds in the latter half, to begin a passage in which the two swap elaborate compliments, begins with an unfortunate comparison (to modern ears, anyway) of his beloved to a horse. She must like it, though, because her language just gets steamier.

It's powerful, powerful poetry from start to finish, as it

traces the relationship of shepherdess and king from courtship through uncertainty to consummation. ("Thus I have become in his eyes like one bringing contentment," says she near the end.[1]) And it does so in such clearly erotic terms that it hardly seems to belong in the sort of Bible most Christians and almost all casual observers of Christianity have come to expect.

Many Jewish people know better, though. Sephardic and Mizrahim Jews read parts of the Song each Sabbath eve as a celebration and reminder of the love of God for the children of Israel. Most traditional Jews also read it during the Passover holiday.

Furthermore, there is no overt mention of God anywhere in the Song. Nevertheless, Rabbi Akiba, considered to be one of the early fathers of rabbinical Judaism, wrote just a generation or two after the death of Christ that "the whole world is not worth the day on which the Song of Songs was given to Israel, for all the Writings are holy and the Song of Songs is the Holy of Holies."[2] And Martin Luther referred to it as "the *High Song*," the name it still bears in German, Dutch, Swedish, and Danish Bibles.

All of them recognized that, far from being a dirty thing, the desire of two people who long, not just for each other's sex, but for each other's *person*, is profoundly godly. After all, we, too, are tripartite beings who express with our bodies the content of our minds and passion of our spirits.

Within the Great Story, there are two primary images of the character of God's relationship with humanity. Perhaps the most dominant is that of Father to child, especially Father to son, the one who inherits all the Father's goodness. That particular image, as we've seen, expands to include the God-Who-Is-Three as an entire holy family opening itself up to welcome orphaned humanity.

The other image is the one that intrigues me now: the Groom, the Heavenly Lover, and the Bride, his Beloved, both consumed by a passionate longing to lose themselves, to fulfil themselves, in each other. It's there in the garden, where the Creator's highest achievement of self-expression is reached in the creation of two gorgeous, naked beings who long to *know* each other (the very apt early biblical term for sexual union). The joining of man and woman in some deep, mysterious way fulfills the image of God in humanity.

"Bone of my bones," Adam mutters, staring astonished at his perfect, brand-new bride. "Flesh of my flesh. She shall be called 'woman', for she was taken out of man."[3]

What a passionate, intimate response! *She was taken out of me—and I will nevermore be complete without her* . . . No wonder Eve fell for him. Somehow he correctly intuited that his first words to this new, entrancing mate needed to be romantic poetry.

The great consummation at the end of the Story, the moment toward which the whole plot has been moving, is the wedding of the Lamb. His bride is the people of God, redeemed and gathered from every time, every people, and mystically built into a beautiful city. God will dwell in that city—inside his precious bride; an image of ultimate consummation if ever there was one.

In between these bookends to the Great Story, I find the wonderfully exciting poetry of the Song, as well as the story of

Hosea and Gomer, together with many other hints, particularly in writings of the prophets, that God longs for union with his people in a way that is romantic, passionate, and . . . well . . . orgasmic.

I am both relieved and excited to find these themes in the Great Story, for my own little story is loaded with sexual desire, both holy and profane, as well as the tensions, ecstasies, wounds, healing, frustrations, and fulfillments that attend it. It's such a constant thread in my life that the only thing more ungodly than allowing it to rule me would be to deny it utterly. To regard my story without considering my sexuality would be to tell, and live, a lie.

In the romance of the Shulamite shepherdess and her king, and in the blazing, prophetic glory of the City of Peace descending from heaven, a bride ready at last to consummate the long eons of her loving, passionate desire for her Lamb, I find hope for my own sexuality. *Her Lamb*—in this context, what a tender, intimate way to regard her man! I hear a hint that, beneath the grotty layers of my selfish lust, there may be a core desire that yet remains holy; that in the most intimate relationship of my life, and in the most uninhibited expression of that intimacy, God is present, and our love is his love.

Many years ago now, my home church commissioned me as a kind of missionary in the urban core of Toronto. My base there was an old building that would soon become home to Sanctuary, but was at the time the meeting place of a small, dying congregation. A couple of evenings each week, I worked with the band, Red Rain, playing various venues around the city.

For most of the rest of the time, I did outreach, alone in those early days, on the streets of our neighborhood. Generally that meant trying to connect with the poor and homeless people who panhandled in the area, but as our neighborhood also included several prostitution tracks, I found myself trying to connect with local working girls too.

The "high track" was where the upper crust of sex workers plied their trade, four streets encompassing one large city block. Some of the women there were quite beautiful, and all of them knew how to wangle every last advantage out of whatever attractive features they had. They were smart, funny, and hard as nails.

It didn't take me long, wandering around those streets late at night, to realize that I was in danger. Not from the women, per se, or their pimps, or the various other rounders that inhabited the dark holes of the city at night. The danger came from within.

Dark thoughts would invade my mind, an almost audible voice that suggested I could do whatever I wanted with these women, *and no one would ever know.* Like almost every male, lust was not a new experience to me. But the images that now flitted through my thoughts were so vivid, and so contrary to what I expected of myself, that I found them truly disturbing. I quickly made a rule for myself: no more walking those streets, at that time of night, alone.

I reflected on this new, uncomfortable revelation of one of the darker corners of my psyche. I had always believed, and still did, that sexuality found its greatest expression within a consecrated love; its purpose, in fact, was the expression and deepening of that love. I had never believed in sex-as-sport, or even as a passing comfort. But these perverse urges were precisely opposite to intimacy. What attracted me most was the idea of sex of the dirtiest kind: my every urge and whim indulged, without any regard at all to the woman involved. In fact, I realized, a necessary part of this scenario was that I wouldn't even know the woman's name, nor she mine. I was repulsed by my own desires, and fascinated at the same time.

My conclusion was that this was not just "sinful" sex, but was in fact *anti-sex*. The antithesis of everything sexual relationship is supposed to be.

Interestingly, my thesis was proved sound within a few years, by which time I had (accompanied by other outreach partners) actually gotten to know some of those women. Now that I knew their names, they were no longer icons of my sordid desires, but human beings. Friends. I could no longer think of them in the same ugly mode. That sickening voice still spoke up occasionally, but now its insinuations just seemed ludicrous, and it was easy to laugh into silence. The antidote, I had discovered, was simple friendship, a kind of brotherly love.

☩

I can imagine old John, the Revelator, staring up into the portentous sky of his vision. He sees a black dot, growing larger as it descends toward him, slowly taking a familiar shape. This thing, massive now, hanging in the sky and glowing with unearthly light, is a city whose walls and gates he recognizes. By some quirk of perspective, he can see buildings within those walls that confirm to him that she is Jerusalem, City of Peace. But while he recognizes her, she is as he has never seen her before: a foundation of gems, gates of pearl, streets of gold, radiant from within. She reminds him of something, or someone from his own past; despite her enormous cubic shape, someone slender, light, and graceful.

And he remembers, this ancient shrivelled man, the moment those many decades ago when he was young and strong, his hands rough from handling the nets. Standing at the foot of a flight of rough stone steps. She descending from the upper floor of her father's house, a vision of beauty and light, reaching as she comes for his outstretched hand.

His bride.

A late summer evening with barely a whisper of breeze. There is a cluster of clouds to the east, but they are of no real concern, as the weather usually comes from the southwest on Lake Ontario. The days are still deliciously long, and we have plenty of time.

The *Hip Hip* is almost forty years old, and showing her age.

Her high, blunt cabin is set far forward atop an awful honey-mustard yellow hull. Her teak rails and other bits of wood trim need refinishing. Her one item of real beauty, a new mainsail so stiff it crackles while being flaked, will remain shrouded this evening. There's not enough wind to fill it.

I love this old boat. I am really only conscious of her shabbiness at this moment because I am handing Maggie down into the cockpit for the first time. Maggie is not shabby at all, far from it. She has all the effortless loveliness that *Hip Hip* lacks. Grace, too: she makes all the right noises about how wonderful my boat is. We motor out of the harbor and across the Eastern Channel, with Bessy, the squat cantankerous inboard engine—six temperamental, low-torque horsepower—burping away beneath our feet. (Is it because boats capture both the compulsive affections and frustrations of men that we instinctively engender them, and everything connected to them, as female?) The water is glassy, rolling toward us a slowly undulating reflection of the city skyline to the west. We tuck in behind the breakwater of the Eastern Gap, in the cove it helps form just off the Ward's Island beach. Maggie takes the tiller while I run forward and drop anchor.

While the sun sneaks down a deepening wall of blue toward the city, growing redder by the minute in excited anticipation of its nightly plunge into the forest of city towers, I light the barbecue perched on the aft rail, and prepare a feast. Salmon fillets, a medley of sweet peppers, red onion, and mango, potatoes sliced and spiced and baking in olive oil.

While it's cooking, we share a glass of wine. Some quiet

conversation, and many lingering looks. By the time we're ready to eat, we have swung gently so that the stern is perfectly aimed at the spectacular panorama of the city, blazing with light, founded on the darkening green line of Ward's Island in the foreground.

We have barely finished eating when we are surprised by a sprinkle of rain. Riding the same backing breeze that swept us stern on to the city, the clutch of clouds that had been huddling on the eastern horizon has snuck up on us. We scamper below, listening to the rain on the cabin roof while still watching the fat red sun as it bends down and sets the CN Tower on fire in the west.

When the rain stops, we reemerge and glance eastward to see whether the rain is truly finished. There is a rainbow. We move together to the foredeck and stand there watching. Maggie's back is against my chest, and my arms are around her. The rainbow is growing: at first just a bright quarter circle, it now arches across the sky. Within minutes, it has become the most complete rainbow either of us has ever seen, beginning and ending in the still water of the far side of the Channel, lacking only a few degrees of an entire circle. The bow of the *Hip Hip* points directly into the center of it.

This, I think now, was the first moment that I knew I wanted to marry Maggie. As spectacular as they were, this conviction was not, of course, just about the immediate circumstances. I've conveyed only something about what we experienced together that evening, and almost nothing about what we communicated to each other. Consummation, and the yearning for it, is so intensely personal and private that it's difficult to express. I can't really begin to describe what my beloved and I desire and find in each other. But I know that it moves in a completely different direction than the subterranean drives unearthed by those anonymous working girls long ago. I know that I desire my love because she is my *love*, and that in desiring her, I desire love itself.

We are profoundly aware, in certain moments of our loving, that the great Lover has entered our little story, and that he is loving us each through the other, and loving us together. This consummation, as fulfilling as it is, leaves us hungering for more, more of each other, more of us together. I want to lose myself in her, and at the same time, I want to encompass her. It seems a paradox, but the more we seek this love, the more truly we become our individual selves.

We cannot yet accomplish the Great Consummation—the purpose, end, and fulfillment of the Great Story. But within our own little tales, as momentary and insignificant as they may be, we are living toward it. The Author, the Great Storyteller, whispers his encouragement.

Who dwells in love, dwells in God.[4]

FIFTEEN

DANCING IN THE NEW WORLD

My Pleasure:

As the Father has loved me, so have I loved you. Now
remain in my love. If you obey my commands, you will
remain in my love, just as I have obeyed my Father's
commands and remain in his love. I have told you this
so that my joy may be in you and that your joy may be
complete.

—FROM THE GOSPEL OF JOHN, CHAPTER 15

Praise be to the God and Father of our Lord Jesus
Christ, who has blessed us in the heavenly realms
with every spiritual blessing in Christ. For he chose

us in him before the creation of the world to be holy
and blameless in his sight. In love he predestined us
to be adopted as his sons through Jesus Christ, in
accordance with his pleasure and will . . .

And he made known to us the mystery of his will
according to his good pleasure, which he purposed
in Christ, to be put into effect when the times will
have reached their fulfillment—to bring all things in
heaven and on earth together under one head, even
Christ . . .

For this reason, I kneel before the Father, from
whom his whole family in heaven and on earth derives
its name. I pray that out of his glorious riches he may
strengthen you with power through his Spirit in your
inner being, so that Christ may dwell in your hearts
through faith. And I pray that you, being rooted and
established in love, may have power, together with all
the saints, to grasp how wide and long and high and
deep is the love of Christ, and to know this love that
surpasses knowledge—that you may be filled to the
measure of all the fullness of God.

—FROM EPHESIANS, CHAPTERS 1 AND 3

Gramps was dancing a jig in Aunt Bette's dining room. If you had only seen a photograph of him, you might assume he was a solemn, humorless man, with his long Irish nose, the horseshoe of steel-colored hair beneath a shining pate, and no-nonsense horn-rimmed spectacles. But behind the specs were eyes that sparkled, and the thin, compressed lips of the photo turned out to be smiling purveyors of a lilting brogue barely touched by almost half a century away from the Old Sod.

Aunt Bette and Uncle Gord were hosting my grandparents' fiftieth wedding anniversary. They had pushed the large dining table against the wall, spread the chairs throughout the living room and tied up the chandelier so nobody would brain themselves. The table was laden with food (all four of the North girls were, like their mother, magnificent cooks), and the modest house seemed jammed with relatives.

For almost as long as they had been married, my grandparents had worshipped with a group of Christians who frowned on dancing, among other worldly, licentious pleasures, but Gramps couldn't help himself. He was delighted, *delighted!* by the party, and because all his daughters and their husbands and all their children were there to celebrate. Had she seen it, my quiet reserved Gramma, she with the core of steel, would have put a stop to the foolishness immediately, I think. But she was elsewhere in the house, so Gramps sang snatches of the jauntiest hymns he could think of, and toe-tapped around the small patch of hardwood floor with his elbows pumping.

I must have been in my early teens at the time, and as

self-involved as is usual at that age. I don't really remember much about the rest of the celebration, but that one moment has stuck in my mind for close to forty years—I was struck by the evidence of his joy. I had some dim realization that it was prompted by a fifty-year journey with his love, and the gathering together here, now, of the fruit of their love. This moment was rich with both experience and potential—the lives of my grandparents, now almost done, had produced a house full of people who had a great deal of living yet to do.

I had always assumed that my mother's Irish parents emigrated to Canada because he was Catholic and she was Protestant.

Richard and Emily North got off a boat at Montreal, a very young, newly married couple, in the early 1920s. One of the continent's oldest cities, it must still have seemed a raw, bustling place to them, with successive waves of European immigrants lapping across the pool of earlier settlers—the French first, of course, then the English and Irish and a smattering of Scots. In Ireland, even most of the families of the "English" gentry had been Irish-born for generations.

Perhaps the polyglot nature of this New World city unnerved them: they boarded a train and headed west. Why they chose to settle in Hamilton, a fierce little steel town clinging white-knuckled to the western point of Lake Ontario, I'll never know. With its rows of smelting stacks fuming skyward, foundries defecating into Burlington Bay, and color everywhere dying slowly beneath a greying soot, it couldn't have been more different from the bucolic downs and pastures of County Athlone.

Both the Norths and Emily's family, the Naylors, were wealthy landowners. Back a few generations, they might have been English gentry themselves. They had farms and pastures, employed tenant farmers, and bred race horses. When Richard reported for his first day of work as a laborer at an appliance factory in Hamilton, the other workers had a good laugh at the bog-trotter who had showed up in a suit and tie.

Because of Ireland's "Troubles," I had concocted a vague and vaguely Shakespearean romance out of Richard and Emily's marriage and emigration: star-crossed lovers separated by the religious antipathy of their noble but rigid families abandon their wealth and heritage to consummate their love; the ire of their relatives forces them to flee forever their native land, and start a new life in the New World . . .

The truth, I learned much later from my grandmother, was more prosaic, but also, in some ways, more beautiful. Although my grandfather's family was so staunchly Catholic that his father essentially gave two daughters to the Church (Richard's sisters were nuns; one, at the age of seventy-odd, cheerfully admitted to my mother that she really hadn't had a choice in the matter), they were also friendly with their Protestant neighbors. The two families often pooled their labor resources at harvest time, reaping first a Naylor field and then a North until all was done.

Now I imagined Emily bringing lunch to her brothers in the field where they bound sheaves alongside the North boys. The antic young Dick North, laughing and liable to sing and dance a lick for no apparent reason; Emily, tall and cool, pretending not to notice. The seeds of unimagined futures—my own among them—planted by their covert glances.

Gramma also explained the real reason for their leaving. Richard was a second son; it was understood that his older brother would inherit the whole of their father's estate. While James would be expected to provide well for his younger brother and other members of the family, Richard would in essence spend his life as an indentured servant to James, receiving an admittedly lavish room and board—everything he and his family would ever need—but no independent income, and no capacity to chart his own course.

So Richard and Emily crossed the ocean, knowing it would be many years, if ever at all, before they saw their families again, to discover who they might become. They dreamed of a family, in its generations, that would fulfil its own diverse and fruitful destinies. They did not flee in fear, but launched outward with joyful anticipation (though alloyed, no doubt, with anxiety and uncertainty) toward a mysterious future that just might grow them into complete, fulfilled human beings.

The consummation of every desire is pregnant with new desires for deeper joys. Each joy is the issue of a long, complex heritage of previous joys and sorrows, failures and victories. Consummation is not merely the slaking of thirst. It's fruitful, fecund, bringing to new life progressively richer pleasures.

In the intimacy of the upper room, away from the crowds that want to co-opt him as a rebel king and, for the moment at least, the politicians who want to do him in, I hear Jesus boil it all down for the eleven men who matter most to him.

Listen, he says.

I know you're worried about what will happen next, and what your status will be when my kingdom comes. But this is not about power, or security, or being important or comfortable. It's about you living with me, and my Father, and the Spirit, in intimate eternal connection.

The many long, tangled threads of human history, your own stories included, have been weaving together to make this one tapestry—the whole of the Great Story is coming to a climax. But not an end—not a finish, but a fulfillment.

It comes down to this: being loved by my Father, and loving you in turn, fills me with joy. And I want that joy to find its utter fulfillment in you. This is it— the ultimate purpose of everything. Through all the generations that are to come . . .

Nobody's life unfolds smoothly, a constant easy pattern of goodness sought and secured. Mine surely hasn't. My grand-parents' didn't. The many consummations we seek are disrupted, deflected, and too often blown to smithereens by conflict, betrayal, loss, illness, accident, or merely our own insufficiency. Often I have sought things that I thought would be good and fulfilling, only to find that they were anything but. Nevertheless, these rhythms of joy-seeking and fulfillments, small and great, roll gracefully from generation to generation, as unstoppable as the swells on a vast ocean.

I desire for my children (and for all the people I have come to love) the same kind of joys I have sought for myself. I pray that their successes will be greater than my own, their failures fewer and less destructive. As much as I enjoyed them as little ones, I am eagerly watching them become fully realized adults; I long for them to discover the particular joys of learning, doing work they love and at which they excel, finding their own unique passions, becoming lovers, partners in life, parents. As I write this, my four kids are in their physical prime, a delight to behold. But I know that there are compensatory joys for those who are aging, so much so that few of my friends who are in their forties, fifties, or sixties would trade the wealth of what the years have made them for a return to youth. While I'll admit I'm in no rush for my children or myself to age further, I do desire for them the accumulated joys of experience. All the while, I'm aware that each consummation toward which I yearn, for myself or for them, is a whispering echo of the great consummation to come.

Especially at the time of important life markers like significant birthdays or anniversaries, graduations or other recognitions of accomplishment, I have the impulse to gather around me the generations of my family, friends, and community members, just as my grandparents did. My joy at whatever it is we're celebrating is deepened by their presence—their joy feeds mine, and mine theirs, until the celebration itself becomes a source of pleasure distinct (though not separate) from the accomplishment or event that brought us together in the first place.

Reality intrudes in a host of ways that obscure this joy, but they don't eradicate it. On the contrary, the fact that, for instance, most families continue to assemble at important moments, despite conflicts and resentments and even outright abuse, proves the immutability of this human and godly impulse to gather together the many strands of our communal story, and to find our individual places within it.

There is an echo here of the voice of God, his breath drifting through me, and through humanity. He is calling us from afar, calling us out of our dark, distant hiding places, gathering together the lost ones, bringing the orphans into the family. This is the One who passes on his name to us, his children, grows us up to look like him, stretching us by many experiences so that we will be capacious enough to begin to know love. So that we might be as "full" as God is.

The image of God as an angry old man huffily bent on

either fixing or smacking down his screwed-up human creations is an enduring one. But that's not the picture Paul or John or the other bards of the Great Story paint.

I love the way Paul stresses that it has been God's *pleasure* from the very beginning to gather us into the family—to adopt us as "sons," that is, inheritors, as the ones who will receive the full scope of the family's wealth, and with it, the future. The mystery of that future, with all that it portends, is God's *great* pleasure—the consummation of the Great Story in the gathering together of "all things in heaven and on earth" into their proper relationship to each other and to their Creator and Savior. A great celebration of the family of God.

John's vision of the New Jerusalem as the place where God will live, surrounded by his beloved children, in harmony with his bride, the jewel of his heart, shimmers with joyful longing. It reminds me of Gramps soft-shoeing around the dining room, warbling off-key melodies, mad with delight at the generations gathered around him, dizzy with excitement at what was yet to come. Pleased with what the years of his own sojourn had brought to life.

On a clear spring afternoon sometime in the early 1920s, the Westinghouse factory whistle blew; moments later, the gates flew open and the day shift came streaming out. Somewhere in the middle of the crowd, perhaps with a new tweed workman's cap pulled down to his eyebrows, young Richard North drifted on the human tide out to Sanford Avenue, wondering absently if he might be transferred from the production of train brakes that were the factory's staple to the rumored new wireless section. "Radio," they called it here in the Americas.

He turned eagerly homeward. The whole city seemed one interminable machine. Could a place possibly be more different from the green fields and dirt roads of County Athlone? There, the sound of industry was the gentle clip-clop of a horse's hooves, the distant good-natured cry of one harvester to another. If you were close enough, the sigh of the barley as it bowed to the scythe. Here, the booming thunder of shunting rail cars, the scream of steam vents, the roar of furnaces. Men shouting to be heard above the cacophony. There must have been times in those early days when the reality of having left the beauty and security of his father's farms for good sat like a sickness in his stomach.

But Emily, tall serene Emily, was waiting. Never a complaint or a question from her, though the whole of their apartment could have fit neatly in the Naylor's parlor. Setting up their household had taken no time at all, and for now she spent her days waiting for Dick to come home. Cautiously venturing alone into the foreignness of this aggressively metallic town to shop for unfamiliar foods, or to do the laundry.

A block away from the factory gate, a man stood on a soapbox on the corner. He must have timed his presence there to the factory schedule, for he waited until the forward edge of the wave of homebound workers swept within a few feet of him before beginning his address. As the first workers slowed to find out what he would say, the rest backed up behind them until, back in the middle of the pack, Richard and those around him were brought to a standstill.

Richard wondered if the man was a communist, or a union organizer. He could not yet distinguish the words, but after a moment or two, most of the crowd started forward again. Some of those at the fore were batting the speaker's words away with dismissive hands, or calling out to him and laughing as they passed by.

As Richard came within range, he realized the man was speaking about God and the Bible—a preacher on a soapbox! He had never seen or heard of such a thing in Ireland. The man was clearly not a priest, for he wore simple workaday clothing and spoke with a natural passion, rather than the remote, measured tones of the pulpit.

By the jostling of the men around him as they muttered their way past, he realized that he had remained rooted to the spot. The preacher paused, smiling at some jibe thrown his way, then turned and seemed to look straight at Richard.

"Come unto me," he called out, holding up a Bible in one hand to indicate he was quoting from it. "All ye who labor, and are heavy laden, and I will give you rest . . ."

I began to realize, long ago in Aunt Bette's dining room, that every consummation of every desire of my grandfather, and all my grandparents and the generations before and after them, profoundly influences who and what I am now. My story is the continuance of a thousand others. Through every generation, God has breathed his invitation to joyful embrace, the very essence of true pleasure. In his arms, every pleasure is safe but thrilling, the dissolution of death and the very fulfillment of life.

Almost all pleasure now is at least potentially dangerous, but no pleasure will be so then. In that perfect joy, nothing will be forbidden, nothing selfish or destructive. Even now, in this poor broken world, every pleasure is an echo of this ultimate joy, each hunger a shadow of true longing for the fulfillment to come.

Gramps and Gramma knew the stories of their own lives, and some of the stories of their parents and children. They understood, in a way that I could not, how the people and events of their lives had played a part in producing the boy who watched his grandfather dance and sing that day. Just so, God has known from before the beginning every choice, every nuance, every longing that would trickle its way from age to age, ancestor to ancestor.

And he has drawn all of them together, consummated them in my own unique person. He knows how all of this will shape my children, and their children. The whole of humanity is imbued with the beauty to be found in every child. Just as he is shaping me, he is shaping the entirety of redeemed humanity, growing us together, and more and more into the full character of his Beloved.

☩

The Spirit who called out to my grandfather so long ago through the street preacher blew gently into the souls of my grandparents. Despite the rigorous religion of the homes in which they had been raised, they had never heard that God desired to know and be known intimately by them, by Richard and Emily. The God of their youth was holy indeed, and remote. A God to be feared and placated. A God to be managed and kept at a distance.

I don't actually know what that street preacher said, or what scriptures he quoted—I admit, I've taken some license in the telling—but I know the essence of what Gramps heard. I know that he heard for the first time in his life an invitation to rest in the arms of God, all his sins forgiven, all his efforts to placate unnecessary. To rest at last, with his head on the Father's chest, and to hear, instead of the angry demand of an impossible righteousness, that gentle voice whispering, *My child, my love—I am so very pleased that you have finally come to me!*

Gramps responded to that invitation as if he'd been waiting for it all his life. It changed his life. The Spirit breathed the same invitation through him into Emily, and from the two of them into the lives of their four girls. The Spirit blew gently through my mother, and my father. He is breathing his sweet invitation still into my own heart:

> *. . . so that my joy may be in you,*
> *and your joy may be full . . .*

EPILOGUE

SKYLIGHT

The skylight is a pearl grey square now, the black filigree of the top leaves of the neighbor's tree etching one corner. Dawn is not far off; an eager bird close by is chirping. I lie in tangled sheets, uncertain how long I've been awake.

Much earlier, after sleepless hours of rolling in one direction, then another, and in slow-motion so as not to wake Maggie, I had finally risen. I stood for a moment beneath the skylight, looking up, trying to sort the half-dreams and racing thoughts that had kept me on the border of sleep. A distant moon blew a precise hole in the night, fired a column of light whiter than bones down through the purple sky. Finally, I completed the ritual, carefully descending the stairs in the dark, avoiding the dog sprawled on the landing, making my way down the hall to the bathroom.

I contemplate doing the same thing again now, not because I feel the urge, but as a means of resetting myself. As Otis does, when he gets up, turns a couple of tight, nose-to-tail circles, and lies down again. I am awake, but not quite awake enough— I find myself drifting, not into sleep exactly, but into thoughts and mental images and the imagination of absurd, alarming situations that are a goulash of fact, fancy, and fear. They've kept me tossing all night.

We buried Sheldon yesterday. My proud Blackfoot brother, my friend these many years; his voice, on many occasions, has been the sound of God breathing into my soul. My unconscious mind, I am sure, is spinning so furiously because it can't quite comprehend that the alcohol has finally killed him dead.

So my night has been a bombardment of splintered memories. Sheldon, a faux far-off look in his eyes, trying to steal the watch from my wrist while he tells me some inane story. The stricken, staring expressions of his street brothers when I turned from the body to say, "He's gone, boys." Them recounting, in tones of puzzled hurt, how only a few hours before they had roused him, half-carried him to the alleyway beside Sanctuary, and laid him tenderly there so that he would be out of the rain. Sheldon laughing, eyes slitted, long mustache hanging down over his joyful open mouth.

I sit up, swing my legs over the side of the bed. Maggie remains motionless, curled up on her side with her back to me and the covers up around her ears.

Him sitting across a table from me, laser-focused, gripping my wrist, speaking words of blessing when I needed to hear them most. In the alley, the deadly bluish white rimming his hands that told me the truth at first glance. The cold flesh of his throat and wrist beneath my burning fingers. Sheldon turning toward me as I step out of Sanctuary's front door; that slow, wide smile as he recognizes me. "It's you," he says. The round of firemen, paramedics, and cops; the long, long wait in a garbage-strewn alley, for the coroner to show up. Lyf and I keeping vigil over the cold husk of Sheldon, tumbled there into a brick and concrete alcove, ravaged by emergency workers with no time for dignity, covered finally by the thin orange blanket. So very present and yet so very *gone*.

Life, I think as I pause again beneath the skylight, is not a stately, straight-line march toward beauty. I could not hear God breathing in that alleyway; no more can I hear him now amid the cacophony of my own thoughts. I get so lost in its minutiae that I can't usually see even my own little story with any clarity, let alone keep track of my place in the Great Story. The extremity or complexity of the moment disrupts the narrative flow, leaves me confused and disoriented, reminds me that I am not the Story-teller. I am *in* the story, not beyond it, and so will have to trust the Author to make sense of it in the end.

Sheldon's street brothers, who stood so shocked in the alley, were pallbearers at his funeral. I was proud, so proud of them, for I know what this cost. They, too, are prisoners of the bottle or syringe. In Sheldon's body they witnessed with terrible acuity the prophecy of that which they fear most for themselves; I could see it in their faces.

Many of my friends from the street are unable to attend memorials, momentarily taken by the very substances that took Sheldon forever. But these men showed up early; they were sober, clean, solemn. They stayed throughout the funeral; they prayed, shared stories of Sheldon, gave gifts of tobacco. They made the long trek to the cemetery, and carried their brother's body to a grave in a flat field beside a highway roaring with thoughtless cars. Their courage in facing the unfaceable gave me a little courage too.

Sheldon's story, as far as his brothers and I can know it, is ended now. But we were part of his story, and he is forever part of ours. We also of each other's, and so on until the expanding web connects us a thousand ways into the one humanity so beloved of God, the one to whom he whispers those affirming, intoxicating, ennobling words.

Passing beneath the skylight on my way back up the stairs, I note that there is a hint of color in the sky now. The leaves on the neighbor's tree are dark green, instead of black. The sun will soon have risen, and so will Maggie. I slide back into bed, exhausted. I lie motionless on my back, hoping that so disciplining my body will impart the inner stillness I crave.

Maggie turns to me, her eyes still closed, and places an arm across my chest. She tucks her forehead into the hollow of my neck and shoulder. She is warmer than I am. I can feel her breath—patient, regular little puffs—at the base of my throat.

Her heat and the rhythm of her breathing are comforting, calming. Her breath is his breath.

My own story is, I hope, far from over. In fact, I do believe that the story I'm living now is really only a small section, or a chapter—maybe just a prologue!—of an eternal narrative, which is in turn one mere thread of the tapestry of the Great Story. Just as I have to step back from the immediate events of my life to get a sense of what's really going on, I've found I must suspend, for the moment at least, the host of niggling questions I have about the Great Story in order to "hear" the whole of it. While I continue to wonder about, for instance, matters of dogma, or historicity, or interpretation, those uncertainties do not keep me from recognizing the broad and thrilling sweep of the Creation, the Fall, Redemption, and Consummation.

The fact that I can recognize these themes in my own little story fills me with humility—my story is so small! Matters that are momentous to me are infinitesimal in the context of the Great Story. I'm also filled with a kind of awestruck pride: the Great Storyteller is recounting his story to *me*, and whispering to me, personally, individually, those beautifully intimate words: *my child, my love, my pleasure.*

I can see the skylight from where I lie with Maggie's head on my chest. The sun is up now: the sky is a living blue, the leaves of the tree like buttered greens in the warm morning light. The bird has been joined by her sisters and brothers in a gentle, contrapuntal song. Maggie stirs, and I know that she is awake, but reluctant to move from our relaxed embrace. She is listening, I am sure, to the beating of my heart, and feeling the breath from my nostrils on her hair. We are silent, and as still as we can be, but we are saying everything that matters to each other.

And I wonder, at the end of this interminable
night, as I am finally able to hear the sound of God
breathing—is my head on his chest, or is his on mine?

ACKNOWLEDGMENTS

The Sanctuary community in Toronto has a lot to do with everything I've ever written for publication. The board of directors grants me the time, the staff are my companions almost daily on this challenging and quickening journey, and Alan Beattie in particular is friend and partner, granting me freedom to write in the first place, then travel around some talking about what I've written. And the people of our diverse community, many of whom struggle with addictions, mental illness, homelessness, and more, are great teachers. The worshippers in our community provide a spiritual home for me unlike anything else I've ever experienced. Dan, Les, and Doug, brothers and bandmates since shortly after Moses came down from the Mount, keep me in the groove, even though I still struggle to sing and count to four at the same time.

My brothers and sisters who are part of StreetLevel, a national roundtable on poverty and homelessness, encourage me constantly to think more broadly and deeply about matters of biblical justice.

As with my last book, Miller and Terri Alloway generously provided time and space away from the usual daily concerns, so that I could actually get down to writing. Their commitment, both before and after publication, is incredible and inspiring. Once again, Tim Huff was my writing buddy, working away in the next room on his own book, *Dancing with Dynamite*, during two writing "holidays," keeping me honest through the day and providing diversionary companionship in the evening. Karen Johnson miraculously got me on a critical flight to Phoenix—a tale too long to tell here.

When first making notes for this book, I polled a number of friends for their takes on the central themes of the Bible. I'm grateful to all for their responses, but especially to Rod Wilson (Regent College, University of British Columbia), who suggested the device of Creation, Fall, Redemption, and Consummation, which provided the structure of the book, and Sister Sue Mosteller (Henri Nouwen Literary Society), who (predictably, if you know Sue) pointed to "intimacy" as *the* great theme of Scripture.

Michael Clarke has been my fellow traveler for many years, helping me hear the words God whispers.

I've never worked with an agent before, and Greg Daniel proved to be a delightful surprise. He not only landed the manuscript with a great publisher, he also provided invaluable and essential editorial advice before submission, when the core concepts were still nebulous and poorly organized. The folks I've connected with at Thomas Nelson are, one and all, a pleasure to work with, and none more so than Bryan Norman, editor. I loved his approach from first contact and not only because he said so many encouraging things. I appreciate both his rigor and his flexibility. Both he and Greg contributed mightily to making this a much better book than it would have been had I been left entirely to my own devices.

Of course, each person mentioned in the book, whether by his or her own name or by a fictitious name, deserves and receives my thanks for the gift of individual stories, which have become such important parts of my own.

Family always plays a huge role in what any writer might produce, one way or another, but particularly so in a book of this nature. Apart from God himself, my mother and father, my brothers John and David, my children, and my wife, Maggie, have and have had more to do with the shaping of my own little story, and so this book, than anyone else. I'm profoundly grateful for each of them.

Notes

Two

1. This is the only anecdote in the Bible in which Father, Son, and Holy Spirit expressly and distinctly appear at the same time. That alone underscores the crucial place of this moment in the great story.
2. Hebrews 1:1–2.
3. John 1:9.

Three

1. Most notably Abraham Kuyper, who wrote about the pattern of Creation, Fall, and Redemption. Exactly when "Consummation" was added I've been unable to discover, although my friend Rod Wilson at Regent College would be happy to claim credit if no one else does.
2. Job 19:25.
3. Mark 10:14–15.
4. 2 Timothy 3:16.

5. See John 20:22, where the resurrected Jesus breathes (blows) on his disciples as a means of imbuing them with the Holy Spirit (literally, *the Holy Breath).*

FOUR

1. Genesis 1:27–31.
2. Romans 8:15–16. A little farther on he says we are also adopted as sons, but more on that later.
3. Hebrews 2:10, 13.
4. 1 John 3:2 NKJV.

FIVE

1. Dad would never have described himself that way. He believed that what he achieved was the result of God blessing his efforts.

SIX

1. If you do a web search on "TULIP Calvin," you'll find all the explanation you need and more.
2. Genesis 3:8.

SEVEN

1. Interestingly, this is exactly what is happening in Toronto, as it has already in New York, Paris, and London. As the city core is regentrified, urban poverty is moving outward. And wealthier people are beginning to think about poverty.
2. Genesis 3.
3. Isaiah 1:5–6, 18, paraphrased.

Eight

1. Isaiah 52:14; 53:2, 3.

2. 80 degrees Fahrenheit.

3. A ceremonial acknowledgment of the need of cleansing, and a purifying act.

4. Galatians 5:11.

5. Galatians 2:20, emphasis added.

Nine

1. In 1994.

2. The Greek tense indicates that he "asked and kept on asking."

3. Mark 5:1–20.

Ten

1. In the movie *Blood Diamond* (2006), written by Charles Leavitt and directed by Edward Zwick. Parallels to the Great Story abound in this otherwise thoroughly Hollywood movie, whether intentional or not: the loving father (Djimon Hounsou) who gives all he has to redeem his family, and especially his young son, Dia, descending into hell and facing "the devil"; the man (Leonardo DiCaprio) without natural parents who, although struggling against it, ultimately gives his life for the lost boy; the woman (Jennifer Connelly) who quietly makes it all possible, operating behind the scenes, and is the voice of conscience throughout. Only by the united effort of this "Trinity" can the lost, enslaved, imprisoned family

of the father be saved. The cost of their redemption is blood—the blood of the man who sacrifices himself, and, lest we miss the point, the Blood Diamond of the title.

2. Job 19:25.

3. "You know that it was not with perishable things such as silver or gold that you were redeemed . . . but with the precious blood of Christ, a lamb without blemish or defect" 1 Peter 1:18–19.

4. Galatians 3:1.

5. Galatians 5:1.

6. Philippians 3:3–11.

7. Paul's use of the word *son* is not intended to exclude women. Far from it—as, in that culture, only sons could inherit from their fathers, he is making the point that all are the same in Christ (Jew, Greek, slave, free, male and female); the redemptive agenda of the gospel is to break down every barrier, every restriction, every prejudice.

8. You can read more about the story of the band, and lots more about the Sanctuary community, in two other books: *God in the Alley* and *The Twenty-Piece Shuffle*.

Eleven

1. Exodus 6:6.

2. 1 John 2:24, emphasis added.

3. The NIV rendering, "Dear friends," is sadly weak. Though long out of popular use, the old term "beloved" expresses the determined focus of tender, passionate affection that the text requires.

Twelve

1. Ephesians 1:4–5, 9.

2. I'm resisting the temptation to write many pages about this, since this book is about hearing God in a very personal, intimate way. Redemption, as a theological concept, and justice, as a social ethos and pursuit, are inextricably linked.

Thirteen

1. Hebrews 2:10–13, author's paraphrase.

2. Exodus 20:5 and elsewhere in the Torah, but see also Leviticus 20:5. The "visiting" of the "iniquities of the fathers" upon three or four generations of their offspring seems mostly to have to do with people leading their families into the worship of false gods.

Fourteen

1. Song of Songs 8:10.

2. Mishnah Yadayim 3:5.

3. Genesis 2:23.

4. 1 John 4:16, author's paraphrase.

Reader's Guide

Part One: The Heart of the Matter

One

The Voice from Above

1. Imagine yourself sitting on the bank of the river, listening to the Baptist shout his message of forgiveness as he plunges men and women into the silty water. How would you have felt about this man from the wilderness, snacking on locusts as he bellowed out his revolutionary message?

2. Jesus stood in the river as the clouds rippled above and the sky breathed upon him, "This is my son. I love him, and I am pleased with him." Has this message turned your ordinary life into something different? Has it clarified your past or changed the direction of your future? How?

3. Sometimes God speaks so quietly his voice is easily missed. What are the noisy distractions in your life, those things that drown out the voice of God?

Two

The Heart of the Matter

4. "It's the work of a lifetime to die to our old life and rise again to new life." How has your story centered on repentance, or changing the course of your thinking about yourself, your world, and your Creator?

5. In his incarnation, and especially in the moment of his baptism, Jesus represents both God and humanity. He is one of us, yet separate from us in every way. How does this aspect of his person impact his message for us?

6. To his beloved, God speaks "in Son." This special language is shared in moments of intimacy between father and child, when we are close enough to feel his breath upon our necks. Why does he choose to speak to us this way instead of through instruction or law?

Three

The Great Story

7. "A good story allows you to admit your fears and hope that you might be a hero in the face of them." What story is God writing with your life?

8. The four movements of the Great Story are Creation,

Fall, Redemption, and Consummation. This "plot outline" helps us correlate our story to the great one. What "act" of the great story do you find yourself in now?

9. All of Scripture is God-spirited. How can reading through his Word help you to feel his breath on your face and to hear his voice speaking intimately to you?

Part Two: CREATION

FOUR
_____

A GOOD LIKENESS

10. Many of us desire to have children or a family, people who are a part of us and upon whom we can lavish the very best of what we have. We desire to connect with someone who will become like us but also clearly himself or herself. Is this desire part of the core of who you are, or do you desire something different for your identity and image?

11. The kingdom of heaven is for those who will come as little children, understanding that we are free to cry out to God as our daddy. Do you find it difficult to view God as a doting daddy? Why?

12. When the Father, Son, and Spirit hovered together over the deep and discussed the crown of their creation, they envisioned a creature who would grow in relationship

with him, so that one day his children would be like him. Are you entering that relationship in the moments that matter?

Five

Happiness Is a Hot Shower

13. "In my youth, I dared to challenge some of the deeply held convictions of the church in which I was raised. This opened a rift in the relationship I cherished with my parents and brothers. But it was their loving and nurturing spirit toward me that gave me the courage to take action in the first place." How did the actions of your youth result from the environment you grew up in, and how did they affect the relationships you value most?

14. "As a young adult, I longed for a verbal reassurance of my father's love, but over time I realized he'd been telling me he loved me in more ways than I had realized." Do you have this same experience with your father, or your heavenly Father, as well?

15. "Living in the love of our heavenly Father is the closest thing there is in this world to living in the garden of Eden, and the clearest picture we have of the glory that is ahead of us." When do you most tangibly feel God's love toward you? In which moments do you feel that you are close enough to hear him breathe?

SIX

HAMMER AND NAILS

16. John Calvin's famous TULIP presentation of the good news starts with a *T* for total depravity, but starts too late, essentially ignoring the foundation of the creation story. What did Calvin omit in his plot outline, and why is it so important for us to remember?

17. "God doesn't need our help to build our redemption houses any more than I needed my preschool son Caleb's help to build the addition to our home when his baby brother was born," so why does he invite us to participate?

18. "God doesn't snicker at our delusion that we're doing Really Important Things. Instead, he slips his arm around us and smiles with quiet delight in his voice." What is he saying to you in these moments?

Part Three: THE FALL

SEVEN

THE BEAUTY OF A BROKEN MIRROR

19. God's voice speaking to us in Isaiah 1:2–6, 18 is not that of an angry judge but that of a loving and agonized parent, his soul torn by his child's rejection, his heart battered by the knowledge that even in the child's tormented state,

the worst is yet to come. When you read these words, do you feel criticism or compassion? Does his pleading make its way into *your* heart, or do you think of others when you read this passage?

20. Humanity often gravitates toward evil, as we see in the lives of Adam and Eve, not to mention the world swirling around us every day. How has evil compounded itself in your life, perverting your desires and actions in a way that offends and hurts God?

21. God's great gift to us is his grace, and our sin is the proving ground for that gift. How has God's grace been proven in your life?

EIGHT

DREAMING OF ME

22. Sacrifices are made on holy ground—the tabernacle, the temple, the Cross. But for many of us, a lifetime of being saturated in these images and this language has made hallowed ground tepid and familiar. Has this been your experience?

23. When you ponder the cross, do you picture Jesus as dirty, gory, and sordid? Or do you seek a safer, more mundane way to witness the embodiment of God's love for us?

24. How does Jesus' condition on the cross comfort us with the knowledge that God loves us despite the darkest truths of our souls?

Nine

Chocolate Rosebuds

25. "We are walking compendiums of bruises and sores, sinful beings rebelling against the one who loves us deeply and passionately." Why would God want to get close to us?

26. Those who lived across the shore from the untameable Wild Man of Gesara probably developed legends and rumors about the man for their own advantage out of fear of his condition. Have you witnessed similar examples of dehumanization in your experience, and if so, how can you bring the gift of humanity and God's love into the lives of those so alienated?

27. God tells us, *My pleasure rests upon you, right here, right now. Not later, right now.* How do you see God's pleasure resting upon you right now?

Part Four: Redemption

Ten

Striking Off the Chains

28. Redemption is the climax of the Great Story, the moment when a new judgment is rendered about something previously thrown aside as worthless. What have

you re-named or re-judged in your life, and what is still carrying the mantle of unworthiness?

29. What gives you hope that you're moving toward the promised land as you travel the seemingly limitless wilderness of this life?

30. How does the long desert of alienation and rejection bring you to the point where you're vulnerable enough to hear the rhythm of the Father's breath?

Eleven

Traveling to Canaan

31. The Exodus of more than a million people, all born into slavery, is one of the foundational narratives of the Great Story. What other stories in the Scriptures hint at God's redemptive agenda?

32. In an era when gods were generally viewed as dangerously powerful, largely amoral, and a little grumpy, what conclusion did the Israelites come to as they traveled their distinctive journey? What chains did they have a difficult time loosing?

33. How, in your experience, has the locus of your suffering become a place of God's glory?

Twelve

Plastic Pop Bottles

34. Jesus died as a common criminal. His followers were a

gaggle of uncouth back-country rabble-rousers, many of whom would be executed. Their center of worship, the temple in Jerusalem, would be razed to the ground. Why is the Great Story told through this group of people whom most would consider losers?

35. What pleasure does God and man find in taking something worthless and making it into something both useful and beautiful?

36. Leonard, the man who escaped a life of boyhood prostitution, has a powerful testimony about the reach of God's redemptive agenda, yet the retelling of his story came to represent a terrible danger to him. How? Is this something you've experienced in your life?

Part Five: CONSUMMATION

THIRTEEN

ABOARD THE *AMADEUS*

37. "The biblical sketches of the end-which-is-a-beginning are mere line drawings, but they give us a hint of the perfect happiness that we will experience when we finally consummate our marriage to the Lamb." Is this landscape something you dream of, or are you hesitant to hope for this future?

38. "I have never met a family in which there was not some measure of alienation and pain, but we long for harmony

in these truly God-given relationships." Can you imagine how God's consummation will occur within those relationships most central to your spirit?

39. In what ways have the children paid the stiffest price for the sins of the parents in your family? Your own child's spirit must be aching in some way, and, if you're a parent, your children's hearts are at your mercy as well.

40. Many people fear the end of their lives, the unknown journey that awaits them upon their passing. But God promises that he is the beginning and *the end*. Does this bring you comfort?

FOURTEEN

EROTICA

41. Why would it be a lie—ungodly even—to regard your story as part of the Great Story without considering your sexuality as part of it?

42. What is the antidote to our perverse urges for sex-as-sport?

43. "In the moment when I knew I wanted to marry Maggie, I recognized that I wanted to lose myself in her and at the same time encompass her." How is it that the more we seek love, the more truly we become ourselves?

FIFTEEN

DANCING IN THE NEW WORLD

44. How have the rhythms of joy-seeking and fulfillments, small and great, rolled from generation to generation within your family? Have those things you've sought as fulfillment turned out to be anything but?

45. "The image of God as a huffy old man bent on smacking down us screwed-up humans is an enduring one," but how is it dramatically different from the one Paul, John and the other authors of Scripture present?

46. When we rest at last, with our heads on the Father's chest, we will hear not angry demands of an impossible righteousness but his gentle voice whispering, *My child, my love—I am so very pleased that you have finally come to me!* When have you heard the distant echo of this whisper, and what do you imagine it will be like when you hear it in perfect clarity?

ABOUT THE AUTHOR

Greg Paul is a pastor and member of the Sanctuary community in Toronto. Sanctuary, a community in which people who are wealthy and people who are poor live, work, and share their experiences and resources on a daily basis, makes a priority of welcoming and caring for some of the most hurting and excluded people in the city, including addicts, prostitutes, homeless men, women and youth, gay, lesbian, and transgendered people. (www.sanctuarytoronto.ca)

A former carpenter, Greg has been involved in inner-city ministry since his teen years. He is the father of four children and married to Maggie, who has three children of her own. He is the author of two other books: *The Twenty-Piece Shuffle* and *God in the Alley*.